5/18/01
1/14/00
(12)
4HT 1JB

THEotherAMERICA

Teens in PRISON

by
Gail B. Stewart

Photographs by
Natasha Frost

Lucent Books, P.O. Box 289011, San Diego, CA 92198-9011

These and other titles are included in *The Other America* series:

Battered Women

The Elderly

Gangs

Gay and Lesbian Youth

The Homeless

Illegal Immigrants

People with AIDS

Teen Mothers

Teen Runaways

Teens in Prison

Cover design: Carl Franzen

Library of Congress Cataloging-in-Publication Data
Stewart, Gail 1949-
    Teens in prison / by Gail B. Stewart; photographs by Natasha Frost.
      p. cm.—(The other America)
    Includes bibliographical references and index.
    Summary: Four teenagers who were sent to prison at an early age
discuss their life in prison and their hopes for the future.
    ISBN 1-56006-338-6 (alk. paper)
    1. Juvenile delinquents—United States—Juvenile literature. 2. Juvenile
delinquency—United States—Juvenile literature. 3. Juvenile justice,
Administration of—United States—Juvenile literature. [1. Juvenile
delinquency. 2. Prisoners.] I. Title. II. Series: Stewart, Gail, 1949–
Other America.
    HV9104.S82   1997
    364.3'60973—dc20   96–44687
                                                                                CIP
                                                                                 AC

The opinions of and stories told by the pe~ l ..... k are entirely their
own. The author has presented their ..... ir own words, and has
not verified their accuracy. Th~ .... ~n make no claim as to the
objectivity of their accounts.

Printed in the U.S.A.
Copyright © 1997 by Lucent Books, Inc.
P.O. Box 289011, San Diego, CA 92198-9011

Contents

Foreword

O, YES,
I SAY IT PLAIN,
AMERICA NEVER WAS AMERICA TO ME.
AND YET I SWEAR THIS OATH—
AMERICA WILL BE!
LANGSTON HUGHES

Perhaps more than any other nation in the world, the United States represents an ideal to many people. The ideal of equality—of opportunity, of legal rights, of protection against discrimination and oppression. To a certain extent, this image has proven accurate. But beneath this ideal lies a less idealistic fact—many segments of our society do not feel included in this vision of America.

They are the outsiders—the homeless, the elderly, people with AIDS, teenage mothers, gang members, prisoners, and countless others. When politicians and the media discuss society's ills, the members of these groups are defined as what's wrong with America; they are the people who need fixing, who need help, or increasingly, who need to take more responsibility. And as these people become society's fix-it problem, they lose all identity as individuals and become part of an anonymous group. In the media and in our minds these groups are identified by condition—a disease, crime, morality, poverty. Their condition becomes their identity, and once this occurs, in the eyes of society, they lose their humanity.

The Other America series reveals the members of these groups as individuals. Through in-depth interviews, each person tells his or her unique story. At times these stories are painful, revealing individuals who are struggling to maintain their integrity, their humanity, their lives, in the face of fear, loss, and economic and spiritual hardship. At other times, their tales are exasperating, demonstrating a litany of poor choices, shortsighted thinking, and self-gratification. Nevertheless, their identities remain distinct, their personalities diverse.

As we listen to the people of *The Other America* series describe their experiences they cease to be stereotypically defined and become tangible, individual. In the process, we may begin to understand more profoundly and think more critically about society's problems. When politicians debate, for example, whether the homeless problem is due to a poor economy or lack of initiative, it will help to read the words of the homeless. Perhaps then we can see the issue more clearly. The family who finds itself temporarily homeless because it has always been one paycheck from poverty is not the same as the mother of six who has been chronically chemically dependent. These people's circumstances are not all of one kind, and perhaps we, after all, are not so very different from them. Before we can act to solve the problems of the Other America, we must be willing to look down their path, to see their faces. And perhaps in doing so, we may find a piece of ourselves as well.

Introduction

Donnie, a fifteen-year-old boy from a poor neighborhood in central Los Angeles, has broken the law dozens of times. From vandalism and curfew violations beginning when he was eleven or twelve to more recent crimes of assault and drug dealing, he is no stranger to the juvenile justice system. Today, after being found guilty of selling crack in the halls of his apartment building, he is being sent to a high-security correctional facility for juveniles.

Across town, another fifteen-year-old is also in trouble with the law. Sharice, a high school sophomore, has pleaded guilty to shoplifting makeup and earrings from a local mall. Like Donnie, Sharice has committed such crimes before. This time, her social worker and the judge have decided to send her to a therapeutic group home. They hope that Sharice will get the help she needs, so that she can return home to her parents.

Unlike Sharice and Donnie, fourteen-year-old Lee has never been in trouble with the police before—until today. He was caught by police as he and another boy were stealing a VCR and an expensive camera from a house. Lee is in the downtown juvenile facility, where he is awaiting an appearance before a judge. A social worker assigned to his case after his arrival at the juvenile facility has advised Lee that it may be a week or two until his court appearance.

JUVENILE JUSTICE

Hundreds of adults will be dealing with Donnie, Sharice, and Lee, as well as the more than 100,000 other juveniles who are in prison on any given day in the United States. Some are lawyers and judges who must handle a juvenile offender's legal case. Others, such as social workers, therapists, teachers, guards, and counselors, deal with the offenders while they are serving time at a particular prison or correctional facility. In addition, follow-up workers, home counselors, and probation officers help the young person make the adjustment to life outside once the time is served.

All of these workers make up what is known in the United States as the juvenile justice system. The system operates on different premises from those underpinning the adult justice system.

"The idea isn't so much that the juvenile offender is punished for his or her crime," explains one juvenile defense lawyer from Chicago. "Because we're working with young people here—in my case as young as ten or eleven—the focus is on changing the behavior that got them arrested in the first place. No matter if it's a relatively minor matter like truancy or a more serious offense like drug dealing or assault, the idea is that these are *kids*. And we've got to make sure that they learn what it is they need to learn.

"Yes, discipline is part of it—a lot of youth offenders haven't had much discipline at all in their lives. But a bigger part is treatment—whatever it takes so the kids can straighten themselves out and live right. The idea is that we never want to see them again in the system—never."

A RELATIVELY NEW IDEA

Surprisingly, the idea of a separate system of justice for juveniles is relatively new. The history of the legal and penal systems for those under eighteen is quite a grim one; its roots go back many centuries.

In twelfth-century England during the reign of Henry II, for instance, no distinction was made between adult lawbreakers and young offenders. All were held in prisons and jails under appalling conditions. Rats, fleas, and roaches infested the space. With the infestation of vermin came rampant disease, especially typhoid fever, an infectious and often fatal intestinal disease worsened by inadequate rations of food and fresh water.

The death rate from typhoid fever for children was already great. Incarcerated children, as well as adults, died five times more often from the disease than did the general population. So many prisoners caught typhoid fever, in fact, that the disease was widely known as gaol fever, since jails, not bacteria, were believed to cause it.

Over the centuries, very little was done to improve prison conditions for young offenders. In the 1500s physical punishment was doled out as regularly to juveniles as to adults. Beggars and petty thieves over the age of fourteen, as one historian writes, "were grievously whipped and burned through the gristle of the right ear with a hot iron."

In the late 1700s, the founding fathers of the new United States, charged with setting up the institutions of government, based the court system on what they were most familiar with—the English system. And in the eighteenth century that system had changed only slightly from the time of King Henry II.

The courts distinguished between children and adults, but the legal perception of adulthood was quite different from modern definitions. Children seven and older could stand trial in criminal court for breaking laws. If they were found guilty, they could be sentenced to the same punishments as adults—including prison and even death.

PARENS PATRIAE

By the middle of the nineteenth century, however, reform movements were beginning to change the way children were viewed in society. Called by some historians the "child-saving age" because of great strides made in education and child welfare, this era was marked by governmental shifts in attitude toward young lawbreakers.

The essential shift was to cease thinking of children as merely small adults; increasingly, the courts concentrated on the juvenile offender more than the crime. By the 1860s, most major cities in the United States maintained separate facilities for imprisoning youth. In 1899 the first juvenile court was established in Cook County, Illinois, based on a concept known as *parens patriae*, a Latin phrase that translates as "the government as parent." Since the actual parents of these juvenile criminals could not control them properly, the reasoning went, it was the duty of the judge to act as parent.

The result was a relaxation of court proceedings, a process in which a judge talked with the child and any interested adults, and then made a decision based on what the judge perceived as the child's best interests. Since the matter of guilt or innocence was of secondary importance, attorneys were not included to try cases.

The judge would decide whether the child should attend a correctional facility known as a reform school, to get an education or learn a trade, or perhaps be placed in a foster home where he or she could get more attention and discipline. Whatever the decision, rehabilitation—not punishment—was the watchword. The length of the "sentence" depended on how quickly the juvenile was rehabilitated or how quickly he or she turned twenty-one, whichever came first.

But by the 1960s, it was becoming clear that the reformed juvenile justice system was not working, for several reasons. As might be any system based on the arbitrary decisions of a single person, the system was riddled with injustice. Youth who were deemed "potential problems" by a judge could be put away for years without recourse. In fact, since the subject of guilt or innocence seemed irrelevant to juvenile trials, many youth were being "sentenced" without anyone proving whether they were even guilty of the offense of which they'd been charged! To many, it seemed obvious that the juvenile justice system needed to be radically changed.

JUVENILE RIGHTS

The late 1960s and 1970s saw many important changes in the way the juvenile justice system operates. One of the most drastic of these changes is that courts could no longer rely on the discretion of one judge without allowing the juvenile the same due process of law that is offered to adults. To protect against further abuses, the juvenile was given the right to an attorney.

The juvenile justice system today is a reflection of that thinking. Although the proceedings are sometimes less formal than adult criminal hearings, safeguards exist to protect a juvenile's civil rights. Trials *do* determine guilt or innocence. Probation officers, law enforcement agents who have an ongoing relationship with the offender, can make recommendations as to the best way to proceed if a juvenile is found guilty, including probation, sentencing to an institution, or some placement in between. Yet despite these changes the juvenile system is more under attack now than ever before. The pendulum is swinging away from single-minded concern for the juvenile offender's best interests, toward the best interests of society.

CHANGING CRIMINALS

The 1980s and 1990s have seen enormous changes in the kinds of crimes committed by juveniles.

"No longer is it just the misdemeanors—the minor stuff that

kids do," says one law official in Minneapolis. "Now we got hard-core felons, some of them I don't think feel a thing after they rape someone, kill someone. It's that way here, it's that way all over the country."

The statistics seem to confirm this opinion. Among the fourteen- to seventeen-year-old segment of the population, homicide arrests have tripled in the past ten years. In 1986, the majority of the cases heard in New York City's Family Court were misdemeanors. In 1995, 90 percent were felonies—very serious crimes such as murder, rape, robbery, and assault.

"It's a scary thing," admits a Chicago police officer assigned to the city's gang unit. "You see kids ten, eleven years old carrying weapons. A lot are involved in gangs and drugs. We've got a whole population of disturbed kids out there, from a lot of single-parent or no-parent families. They're mad and bored, and they don't have anything to lose. And so we read about the eleven-year-old here in Chicago spraying a group of girls with an automatic weapon, killing one of them. And we hear about the kid out East who hammered a bunch of nails into some little kid's heels. And the thirteen-year-old who raped a neighbor lady.

"The list just keeps on growing. Just when you think these are just sensationalist headlines, you see a whole handful of the same kinds of cases in your own city. It's real, real scary. These kids aren't even like real kids. They're without remorse, without sorrow."

AS ADULTS, WITH ADULTS?

Many people feel the trouble lies with our juvenile justice system, which has always placed a high priority on rehabilitation. The problem is not that some juveniles cannot be rehabilitated, say critics, but that the government is wasting money and resources dealing with offenders who have no interest in changing their ways.

"We need to throw out our entire juvenile justice system," says Gil Garcetti, district attorney for Los Angeles County. "We should replace it with one that both protects society from violent juvenile criminals and efficiently rehabilitates youths who can be saved—and differentiate between the two."

Another expert on juvenile crime agrees. "The young have learned an ominous lesson [from juvenile institutions]: They can get away with breaking the law indefinitely with hardly a risk of swift, sure, and stern punishment."

10

The solution, many think, is to start treating violent juvenile offenders more like violent adult offenders. And some states are already moving in that direction by lowering the age at which juveniles may be tried as adults. In 1994, for instance, California governor Pete Wilson signed a bill lowering that age to fourteen.

But there are those who, while conceding that the present system does not work, are worried about treating our youngest criminals as adults. Confining juveniles in adult prisons, they argue, would be too dangerous. Sexual and physical abuse are common in prisons, and the younger prisoners would be vulnerable targets. They worry too that shifting the focus to punishment would take valuable funds away from the juvenile institutions and services that desperately need them for rehabilitative programs.

"I still think down deep, kids can change," one social worker insists. "I would hate for us to go back to the old days when you had eight-year-olds being hanged and tortured. But the mood of this country—and believe me, I can understand the frustration—seems to be more interested in society's safety than in turning around the life of a kid. I just think that's too bad. So many people have given up on these kids, since they were little. And now, we are doing the same thing."

LOCKS AND BEEPS

The juvenile justice system in the 1990s is a hodgepodge of ideas. State laws vary even in the basic goals of juvenile justice. In a 1991 survey, one sociologist found that almost an even three-way split exists among states whose goal was punishment, states whose goal was rehabilitation, and states that favored some combination of the two.

Juveniles arrested for a crime cannot be certain what will happen to them once they are taken to the police station. States have nowhere near enough money to try every juvenile who is arrested. After being processed (fingerprinted and photographed, in addition to having personal data put on record), the juvenile may be placed in a juvenile center. This type of facility serves as a short-term lockup for offenders awaiting a court hearing. In many cases, especially for a first-time offense, a juvenile may be released into the custody of his or her parents, without spending much time at all at a juvenile center.

Some juveniles who are found guilty at their hearings are

sentenced immediately; others wait at the juvenile center until placement is determined. Often it is a matter of space—many of the alternatives open to a judge are unavailable due to being full, so days or even weeks may go by until a suitable situation is found.

The alternatives for placement differ widely. Some offenders, especially those with a history of violence or poor outcomes in previous placements, may be sent to a correctional facility or juvenile prison. Although such facilities are almost always secure, or locked, they offer a wide variety of opportunities for youth to get an education, job skills, therapy, and counseling.

For less violent offenders, a less secure group home or ranch experience can be sought. Typically this consists of a small group of juveniles who live under one roof, go to school during the day, and work (either by doing chores or holding outside part-time jobs) after school hours. Many social workers think that group homes and ranches can be good intermediate steps between prison and freedom.

House arrest is a form of incarceration that is being used widely in many states. Police monitor juvenile offenders through an electronic beeper placed on an offender's ankle and a monitor in the house.

"You aren't allowed to leave the house—if I get too far away from the monitor in the kitchen, it sets the beeper off downtown," explains one teen interviewed in this book. "And believe me, you don't want to do that. The police call, and the squad car comes over, and if you're not there, you are in deep trouble. They scramble your phone so it makes weird noises after a couple of minutes—that's to keep you off the phone, so that if they want to call you and check on you, they'll always be able to get through. In some ways, being at home on house arrest is worse than being locked up at juvenile center, because you get teased into thinking you're free, when you really aren't!"

No Such Thing as Typical

In *The Other America: Teens in Prison*, four young people—each with experience in the juvenile justice system—tell their stories. Some have been confined in high-security lockups; others have spent time in group homes or under house arrest.

Their stories differ as much as their experiences in the juvenile justice system. Maniac, a former gang member, recently finished a prison term for assault. "It could have been for dealing drugs or weapons, or anything," he admits. "It was the assault that I got caught for."

Martin is a sixteen-year-old under house arrest. He was caught two months ago robbing a house. After his release, he will go to a correctional facility far from home for several months, hoping to do well and return home. Martin says that his experience with the justice system has convinced him he will never commit a crime again.

Kara is a seventeen-year-old girl who has experienced almost every type of "prison" the state has to offer—therapeutic group home, juvenile center, long-term correctional facility, and house arrest. Her crimes are "status offenses"—acts defined as criminal only because she is a minor. Running away, she says, has always been her main crime, but "when I'm eighteen in a few months, it won't be a crime anymore."

And there is Marvin, perhaps one of the biggest success stories of the juvenile justice system. A sixteen-year-old who started out selling crack as a little boy in Chicago, he graduated to gang activities, assault, and drug dealing. After being thrown out of his mother's house for fighting with his cousin, Marvin went first to juvenile center and then to a ranch. He is now a star basketball and football player, as well as a 4.0 student, and is confident that he is a changed person.

The most striking characteristic of these four young people is that there is no "typical" juvenile offender. Each has a different attitude about his or her life, and different ideas about the future. Some feel they are better off for the experience, while others view it as an enormous waste of their time. Race and economic levels differ, too. The only thing that they truly have in common is their feeling about being confined.

"No matter if you got a monitor on your leg or you're in some high-security lockup," says one. "You're still doing something you don't want to be doing. You're still living by somebody else's rules, and doing what somebody else tells you to do. They can call it anything they want, but it's still prison."

Maniac

"I MEAN, NONE OF US WAS GOING
TO GET OUT OF THERE [THE
JUVENILE PRISON] AND RETURN
TO A PERFECTLY FAIR WORLD, OR
ONE THAT DIDN'T HAVE PROB-
LEMS. SO THEY HELP YOU LEARN
TO DEAL WITH THE PROBLEMS
AND THE UNFAIRNESS."

"My real name isn't Maniac, no," he says with a smile. "It's
Charles. But everyone, maybe except one or two people in my
life, calls me Maniac."

He is sitting with a visitor on the front porch of his house. The
neighborhood shows signs of once having been a nice one, with
large shady trees and large wooden houses. In recent years, however, the area has seen more than its share of murders and gang
drive-by shootings, to which Maniac can attest.

"Yeah, this is a big gang neighborhood," he says, nodding across
the street. "Over there in that yellow house, there's Vice Lords.
Right there is Crips and GDs [Gangster Disciples]. It's maybe not
the best place to live, especially for little kids. But usually the gang
stuff happens other places. These guys take their activity elsewhere.

"Myself, I'm cool with a lot of people. I tell them, 'I'm cool with
you, but don't you be coming over here by yourself, because some
of the people I'm with can't see that.' So I can't keep people safe,
just 'cause I want them to be safe, you understand?"

This said, he walks slowly back into the house to get a sweatshirt. When he comes back outside, he is yawning, although it is
almost noon. He pulls a velour Nike sweatshirt over his head and
sits down again.

"I got no schedule these days," he explains. "I been sleeping pretty late, I guess. Soon that'll change, because I'm about to start looking for a job. See, I've been locked up. I don't mind talking about it, either. I think I'm a different person now than what I was before, so I don't think I got anything to be ashamed of.

REMEMBERING CHICAGO

"I've been locked up in a couple of places—actually more than just a couple," he says. "Just now I got out of a prison for youth offenders. Before that I was in a group home out in the country. But before that, I guess I've been in some other situations, like foster homes. You couldn't really call them prisons or nothing, but if you want to say that my freedom was taken away, then yeah, I was in prison."

Maniac says that although his time in the juvenile justice system began five years ago when he was thirteen, there has never really been a time in his life when he wasn't close to trouble.

"I'm not complaining," he says with a shrug. "I mean, that's the way it is. Where I am from is the south side of Chicago, where things are way different from the way they are in this city. I didn't live there long, but I remember enough to know I didn't like it much. I don't remember too many good things, other than we had relatives there.

"But I remember real good how I would get robbed all the time, just walking down the sidewalk and getting robbed for fifty cents. Just minding my own business, you know, being a little kid. And getting grabbed from around the corner, with a gun getting stuck in my head, and getting told to give them money. It was just kids, just bigger kids.

"I started school back in Chicago, but I don't recall much about that. It was something I didn't like, I guess, since I skipped all the time. I don't think I really had anything better to do than just hang around. There were usually lots of other kids to hang around with in my neighborhood. I didn't really go to school much at all until we moved up here, when I was about eight."

"I NEVER CARED FOR HIM"

Maniac's family consisted of his mother and stepfather and his six brothers and sisters.

"He wasn't no father to me," says Maniac, without expression, of his stepfather. "I guess I call him my dad, but he wasn't. He

15

Maniac's childhood was marred by his stepfather's abuse: "I'd get beat for dropping macaroni on the floor, stuff like that. He'd use belts, extension cords, broomsticks."

was my younger brothers' and sisters' dad, but not mine. I never cared for him; he used to beat on me. I got beat on more because I wasn't his, but he beat on all of us, yes. I'm the oldest, so I guess he figured I was the one who could take it.

"There didn't seem to be no reasons. I mean, it wasn't like there was a need for it. I'd get beat for dropping macaroni on the floor, stuff like that. He'd use belts, extension cords, broomsticks. I got marks on the back of my head still from the broomsticks. And sometimes he'd get tired of hitting me, and just throw me downstairs. This was back in Chicago, but he still kept on doing it when we moved up here. Wherever we went, he'd still be beating on us."

What did his parents do for a living? Maniac shakes his head.

"They didn't do nothing. My dad didn't have a job, at least nothing regular. He just got little off-the-wall jobs sometimes, I guess. Mostly I remember him just sitting around, not doing much of anything. And my mom was busy just staying home with kids. At least, that's what she did for a while, until we came here. When we came here, that's when everything started really going bad."

ELENA

The family's move to Minneapolis occurred because of a death in their family. It is something that Maniac has had trouble dealing with "almost my whole life," he says.

"My little sister died when I was eight. She died of crib death," he says, taking a deep breath, "and I'm the one that found her dead. Her name was Elena, and she was only about four or five months old, pretty little. I remember the day really good. Too good, I think, because I used to really think about it a lot.

"My mom was cooking toast. She'd already made the eggs and bacon and was making the toast to go with it. She said, 'Charles, go get up little Elena.' So I went in there and grabbed her. And her arm, it was stuck, crooked, like this." He curls up his arm, demonstrating. "And the other one was, too. Her mouth was open, and I looked and her tongue was rolled way back in her mouth.

"I was just, like, 'Hey Mom, she's dead.' My mom was, like, 'No, she ain't. Stop playing.' And I'm, like, 'Yeah, she's dead.' And my mom was still yelling at me to stop saying that, but I told her, 'She ain't breathing, Mom; she's dead.'

"So my mom came in there and then saw that Elena really was dead. She just broke down. And then my dad, my stepdad, he snapped, too. Everything just went kind of berserk in the house. Me, I just sat on the couch and watched the whole thing. It didn't affect me right away. I mean, I knew my little sister was dead, but I really didn't know how I was supposed to act or anything."

Maniac says that he wasn't allowed to attend the funeral, because his family worried that it might be too difficult for him to handle.

"Everyone thought I'd go crazy, I guess," he says. "I wasn't allowed. But I heard that at the funeral something really bad happened: They dropped the little casket she was in, and she fell out of there. My dad jumped up and brushed her off and put her back in. Man, I'm glad I wasn't there to see that. My dad had to be helped out of there afterwards. I heard about it from my family, the relatives that were there.

MORE FAMILY PROBLEMS

"Our family moved then, moved from Chicago to here. Maybe it was to get away from that place, since it had bad memories attached to it now. But my mom really changed after that. See, all along, I think my dad was doing drugs. I mean, I couldn't say for sure how long, but I think that. But then he got my mom started on them—mostly crack, yeah.

"Things were different. We were kept out of her room; food would be brought to us, but we didn't eat together. We had TV and everything. We were just supposed to be away from her. She was doing her drugs, and she wasn't ready to be a mother, if you know what I mean.

"How did she act? Not mean or anything, just like she wasn't there. She wasn't interested in us. My dad, you couldn't tell. We'd never been close or anything, so he wouldn't care less about me. I don't think he ever cared about me in the first place.

"I'd go off to school in the mornings, and I was on my own. I didn't care much about school in this place either, but I went more often. I'd go late, though. I'd go real slow in the mornings just so I could miss the bus on purpose. I wanted to walk. I guess in those days, when I was eight or nine, I couldn't see much point in going. Nothing seemed too important to me then."

The family moved back to Chicago for a short time to help out Maniac's aunt. "She was real upset, because my cousin—her son—had gotten killed there. It wasn't no gang thing, no. He was just taking out the garbage one night when somebody just killed him. They were doing target practice. That's what the police said. They said some dude just yells, 'Watch me shoot this nigger in the back,' and then he shot my cousin. So that's why we went back, to help out the family."

Maniac says it was ironic, since his own family was in such turmoil. How could they have been much comfort to anyone else?

18

The death of Maniac's infant sister plunged his mother into drug abuse. Using crack left his mother indifferent to Maniac and his siblings.

"My mom was doing drugs worse than ever. My dad was hardly ever around. And when we came back to Minneapolis, the family was really falling apart. I mean, nothing was working. We kids didn't have no clothes. I mean, we were outgrowing stuff, and there was nothing to wear. We were out of socks, and nobody had shoes that fit.

"I was cooking all the meals, too. I'm a good cook. Back when I was little—before Elena died—I used to hang around home, watching my mom cooking. I liked watching, and I must have learned, too, because I made pretty good meals for my brothers and sisters. We had chicken, rice, gravy, biscuits. Real food, nothing from a can. And my brothers and sisters liked it a lot."

Although he was able to help in some ways, Maniac found that emotionally he was not very strong himself. "I was by myself, usually," he says. "That's why I think it didn't bother me that we were going back and forth from here to Chicago. I didn't care about leaving friends because I wasn't really making any. That was okay with me.

"I used to just sit and think, not do much of anything. I mean, the ages of ten, eleven, twelve, I don't really remember much. I watched TV. I know I thought about a lot of crazy things. Like how it would feel to kill somebody, how it would feel to break somebody's neck. Stuff like that. Crazy things a normal person wouldn't think about, I guess. Like, what it feels like to die. I really thought about that a lot.

"Anyway, I wasn't doing much except cooking for my brothers and sisters. I couldn't do nothing about the shoes and the clothes. And I couldn't be at home all the time, either. And so, all of us told about what was happening at home. I went first—told my counselor at the school. And then they talked to my brothers and sisters and found out that they were saying the same as me.

"The next day Child Protection or somebody came to the house and got us, and we got taken away. At first all of us went to foster homes, but none of us liked it. I didn't want to be in no foster home, that's for sure. I kept running away, and I told them I'd keep running as long as they kept me there. I wanted to be with my family, all together. I just wanted them to help my mom so she could get better and take care of us.

"We have grandparents that live around here. They're divorced. Anyway, they let me and my two brothers live with my grandfather, and my grandmother got my sisters to live with her. So that worked out okay, for a while."

SOMETHING TO DO

It was at age thirteen that Maniac was first arrested and placed in the juvenile justice system.

"I was hanging with some friends," he says. "I was just walking along downtown with them, not having much on my mind, I guess. We were fooling around, just looking for something to do. Nothing bad, you know, just like lots of teenagers do.

"So we came across this truck, and we set it on fire. It wasn't my idea, it was my friend Lee's. But I was right in there with them, saying, 'Yeah, let's do that.' It wasn't even at night; it was the middle of the afternoon. Pretty dumb, thinking about it now. So we set the tires on fire. We didn't think it was going to be no big deal. I had found this envelope while we'd been walking through an alley. It had some blueprints in it. So we just took a lighter and got the blueprints burning under the tire, and that started it.

Maniac cooked for his younger brothers and sisters as his mother's drug problem worsened, but he could do nothing to replace their outgrown clothes and shoes.

"Nobody saw us while we were doing it. We were just sitting there for a while, watching it burn and throwing paint cans and stuff, watching them explode when we tossed them in the fire. See, it was a secluded area, where they were building something, I guess. Anyway, when we left, a guy who was going by saw us and called the police. The police came, and we told them we had nothing to do with it, but another police car that had been coming, too, had seen us throwing stuff out of our pockets—our lighters, matches, a knife, stuff like that. So it didn't take no genius to figure that we were the ones that did it."

THE JUVENILE FACILITY

Maniac and his friends were taken into custody and were transported to the juvenile facility downtown. "If you want to know if I was scared, the answer is yes," he admits. "I mean, you try to act all tough at first, you know. I was trying to be brave, act like none of that stuff worried me. So all the way over there in the police car, I was, like, 'Hey, nothing scares me; this is fine, whatever.' But when I got there, I was scared, yeah. I felt like I really needed to get home.

"My grandfather is the one I called, since I was living with him. And I could have come home maybe the same day, only my grandfather wouldn't come and get me. He told me I should stay in jail, that it served me right. A few days wouldn't hurt me, he said. Afterwards he told me he was real upset with me for hanging around those guys. He told me that from then on I couldn't hang with them."

Although the facility was only for juveniles, Maniac insists that it was no different from a jail.

"At first, when you walk in, it seems really big," he remembers. "They have you handcuffed. They check you over, make you take off your shoes, and take your coat. They go through all your pockets—make sure you don't have no drugs or anything. They strip you down and you have to take a shower."

Why take everyone's shoes?

"They don't want you walking," he says. "I guess they figure even if you get out of your locked room, through all those locked doors, you aren't getting far if you have just socks on. Anyway, after the shower, they give you some county blues. They're like surgical clothes that doctors wear. And they put you in a section, called a mod. It's like a living area, and off of that you got your

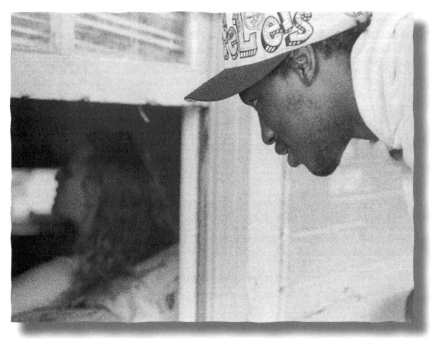

Maniac was first arrested at thirteen for setting a truck on fire with some friends. Although he tried to act tough as the police brought him to the juvenile prison, he admits that he was scared.

own little room. In a mod, there are, like, sixty prisoners, at most. Girls are in a whole separate mod; they're apart from the boys."

LIFE IN THE MOD

Maniac and his friends were charged with second-degree arson and were separated from one another in the facility.

"They didn't want us talking to one another, getting a story figured out," he says. "I guess that makes sense. But really, you can get around that in jail. Just tell someone else to tell your friend such and such. I guess there's no preventing stuff like that from happening except by keeping you locked up all the time, and this place wasn't set up like that.

"See, at first when they put you in your mod, they make you stay in your room for an hour, just locked away in there. In my mod there were twenty other people, but at first I couldn't have nothing to do with them. I didn't even see them. So I sat in my room, feeling kind of nervous.

"After a while, they let you come out into the living area, and the staff goes around to each one and tells you the rules. They got this big black book, and they read the rules to you. There weren't any surprises as far as rules go, no. No cussing, no gang-banging, no fighting at all, no war stories, stuff like that. Nothing to cause conflict while you're there."

Maniac says that coming into the mod helped him over his nervousness, for there were people there he knew.

"I was surprised," he says. "I saw one or two I knew. I mean, they weren't like close friends or nothing, but I knew them. That calmed me down a little. So I started acting really tough again, just so kids wouldn't mess with me; they'd know I was hard. They'd be, like, 'There goes Maniac. Maniac is right there.'

"That was cool. Nobody there knew me by my first name. That's still pretty much the way it is, like I said before. I don't want people knowing my first name, Charles. See, people like to run off at the mouth about things, and I don't want them knowing too much about me. I like the name Charles. I mean, I ain't embarrassed or nothing. I just like to be a little bit of a mystery, I guess."

RACISM

Maniac says he was not surprised at all that many of the staff workers at the jail were unpleasant. "They weren't just unpleasant," he says. "They were jerks. Lots of them were racists, too, and I'm not just saying that. Maybe half were trying to be cool, but they can't be very successful, because of those racist coworkers. I'm serious."

How did he know the staff was racist? Maniac rolls his eyes.

"Listen, you don't even have to ask that. Man, just look at the way black kids were treated, compared with white kids. Some of the staff even use racial slurs: 'nigger' this, 'coon' that, shit like that. When we just jump up and tell them to keep still, they get mad, and we get in trouble.

"A couple of us tried to talk to the cool guys on staff, told them that this was happening. We had the whole mod agreeing that stuff was happening. But they say we have no proof. We had eyewitnesses, but they didn't care. Hey, we had all the white kids in the mod swearing it was going on, but no one listened. And I got mad, really mad.

"I told them, 'Listen, if I shot somebody and one person came forward as a witness, that'd be enough proof for y'all. But how come we all say those guys are calling us nigger and you won't listen? How come you won't believe us? We got the whole mod. Isn't that enough for you to prosecute those guys?' But no, they didn't change their minds. It really made me mad."

PROBATION

At Maniac's trial, the charges against him were dropped down to being an accessory. The witness who had reported the fire, he says, told the police that Maniac was standing and watching while the others were participating.

"My friends had tried to put the whole crime on me," he says, "but that guy told the truth. And it *was* the truth. I didn't set no fire. But I was an accessory because I didn't stop them from doing it. That was fair. So my friends got more jail time, and I got probation, which meant that I was going to go to another foster home.

"I could have gone back to my grandfather's house," he explains, "but he had cancer real bad then and was too sick to do much to take care of me. So I went off to a foster home, which I ran away from, just like before. Then they were going to send me to another foster home, and I told them, 'Look, I'm going to keep

While in the correctional facility, Maniac says he and other inmates encountered racist staff members. Despite their complaints, the matter was never investigated nor were the staff members punished.

running away. You do whatever you got to do, but I'm not going to no foster homes.' So I got sent to a group home. And I was there a long time—two and a half years!"

The group home that Maniac went to was a house with room for about fourteen juvenile offenders. Its mission was to help its clients by providing a stable, consistent environment and by offering counseling to help them deal with the problems that got them in trouble in the first place. However, Maniac says, the whole situation was a difficult adjustment for him.

"I didn't like anybody at first," he admits. "There were about eleven or twelve of us there. The youngest one was thirteen. The lady that ran the thing, she was okay, but that was about it. And the staff knew it. I mean, I wasn't easy to deal with at all. When I first got there, I was, you know, 'f——you,' and 'you ain't my mama,' and stuff like that. I didn't want anybody telling me what to do. I was mean, and I was willing to fight anybody to prove it.

"I tried getting away with stuff at first, breaking as many of the rules as I could. There weren't as many rules as at the jail. I mean, it wasn't really a lockup situation, but it felt like it at first. I had to keep my room clean, do certain chores that were assigned to me, stuff like that. What chores you did always changed. Sometimes it was washing dishes or raking the yard, cleaning the dining room, sometimes, sweeping and mopping the bathrooms.

"But otherwise, if I wanted to talk on the phone or something, that was cool. If I wanted to go outside and throw a football around, that was cool. Like the staff said, just obey the rules, do your chores, and you'll be fine."

TALKING THROUGH PROBLEMS

Maniac says that even though he gave the staff a hard time, he really respected them, even at first.

"I just didn't like them ordering me around. That was the whole deal," he says. "When I got mad, though, they'd just say, 'Chill out; come talk to me.' Stuff like that. Nobody got mad back. They'd pull me over to the side and talk to me real quiet. That's better than, like, highlighting me, picking on me in front of people. That kind of thing was always the stuff that made me violent. I'd get wild if someone did that. But here, they just talked real quiet. I noticed that right away."

Maniac often rebelled against the staff of the group home he spent time in. However, he says, "Nobody got mad back. They'd pull me over to the side and talk to me real quiet."

He *did* get into a few fights when he was there, which was strictly against the rules, and one fight almost got him thrown out of the home.

"The fights were just with other kids, never with staff," he says. "And it was always about something stupid, too. Like one time I fought with this kid, Joe, in the laundry room. He said something to me, and I just slapped him. Then he rushed at me, and I punched him a couple of times and threw him in the dryer. Then I ran upstairs and played like I was just innocent, just browsing through the telephone book or whatever.

"Anyway, Joe came upstairs real mad, ready to fight again, and he grabbed me. I shoved him, only I didn't know the stairs were right there, and he fell down the stairs and hurt himself. It looked to everyone like he started the fight, though. But the staff got to the bottom of it and found out I threw the first punch. For that they were going to send me to another lockup. I was kind of nervous.

"But it all got talked out. Everybody got a chance to talk, and they ended up keeping me there. I just did a lot of extra work.

They knew better than to make me apologize, I guess. They must have known that back then I didn't apologize to nobody."

STAGES OF TRUST

It was important in this group home that the clients could earn privileges and trust, something that many of them had not experienced much in the past.

"They did it by having stages," he explains. "Stage one is when you first get there; things are pretty tight. Stage two is when you can leave—go home for the weekend. Stage three is when you can leave pretty much when you want to. You just have to let the staff know ahead of time. And the last one, stage four, can be two different things. You can be at home, or you can just leave when you want without even telling anyone.

"I was on stage two when I got to go home for the weekend one time. My grandfather died while I was at the group home, and I got to go for the funeral. My whole family was there. I took one of the staff ladies with me. She came to my family's house and everything. I got some tapes and stuff that I wanted to bring back with me to the home.

"It was really nice to be home, even just for a day. I know it was a sad day, with my grandfather dying and everything, but it was nice to be home. It wasn't a sorrowful day for me, because I got to be with my family for a little while."

RUNNING AWAY

When he had earned the trust level at stage three, Maniac ran away from the group home. "It's hard to explain why I ran," he says. "I guess peer pressure. Some kids wanted to get away, and I just went along. I had access to get a ride from there because I had earned that much trust. So I left, and stayed out for a week.

"I didn't really go anywhere secret. I went home, stayed with my family for a little while, and then slept at my homeboys' houses, just friends. Most of them had joined a gang by this time, the Vice Lords. Anyway, I stayed with them. I figured if I stayed at home too long, the people at the group home would find me. So I moved around. I saw all my relatives, though—just stopped in and said hello. I saw my sisters and brothers.

"And after about a week I called them and told them that I wanted to come back. I told them I'd just been messing around, that I had to do it. I just needed to get home, I said, and visit some old friends. They were real nice about it, and let me come back. I made it back up to stage two in just two weeks. I didn't do no home visits, though. I was kind of worried that maybe I'd be tempted to run again."

Maniac was wise to worry about that possibility, although not wise enough to avoid it. Just weeks after coming back to the home, he ran again, this time for good.

"I joined up with my old friends, the Vice Lords," he says simply. "I ended up being one of them. I was always wanting to be with them anyway. I figured I might as well go along and join them. I was out almost a year, just kicking it with my 'homies,' being back in the city. At the time, I felt like I was right back where I really belonged."

GANG-BANGING

His life with the Vice Lords couldn't have been more different from what his life was like at the group home.

"I was gang-banging, pure and simple," he says. "I was selling

After running away from the group home to spend time with friends and family, Maniac returned, only to run away again soon after and join the Vice Lords.

drugs. I even had my own house. Of course, I had somebody older sign the papers because I was underage. But hey, I was making plenty. I made more than enough to pay the rent.

"At first I was just selling other people's drugs, like the BGs [baby gangsters] do. Then after a while doing that, I would buy me enough to sell to my own customers. I was making, like, six or seven hundred dollars each day. I had no problem spending it, either, let me tell you. I had a girlfriend then. Not the one I have now, but man, she had all the things she wanted. She always had stuff. I had my hair done every day. I bought starter jackets, shoes, food, anything I wanted.

"And I was gang-banging, too, beating people up. I had to if the guys I was selling to didn't bring my money back to me. I had to do this, do that—like being a supervisor, you know? I did have guys that would beat people up for me, but I could always take care of my own business. I had lots of guns, always carried one. I led a dangerous life then, shooting at people, getting shot at. I got stabbed, got myself shot in the leg once, that's all. But it was dangerous."

Did he ever question what he was doing? Did he think about the right and wrong aspects of his activities then? Maniac shakes his head.

"Not ever," he says. "Not ever, ever. See, I didn't think about much value, where I was concerned. If I died, I died. I didn't look at no whole picture, nothing like that. If I died, then someone else took over my business.

"I maybe thought about my brothers and sisters, maybe a little. Sometimes I missed them, I guess. I didn't think too much about stage two, three, or four. I don't remember thinking, 'Gee, those staff people at the group home would be disappointed or angry.' My morals or whatever—it was just the gang—whatever we were doing was just what we were doing. That's all."

BACK TO JAIL

Maniac was arrested again a year after he left the group home. The charge was not drug possession or sales, as one might predict. Instead, he was arrested for fighting in what he says was a racial brawl.

"I wasn't even in the city," he says. "I was up in Duluth, way up north. I was visiting my one half-brother who was up there

As a drug-dealing gang member, Maniac led a violent life—beating up people or shooting at them. The violence was also reciprocated: Maniac was stabbed and shot in the leg.

going to school. I'd gone up there to kind of get away from the stuff in the city, just to chill a little. I'd been up there a couple of months when it happened.

"I was by myself one day, walking around with not much to do while my brother was in classes. I walked by this high school. Six or seven of these guys came out, and they were, like, 'Hey, nigger, what you doing around here?' Stuff like that. Telling me to go back to the city where I came from. Anyway, I stopped and just looked at them, and one of them was ready to fight me. The other ones thought I had a gun, which I didn't, and were too afraid.

"Anyway, I was winning the fistfight, and some other dudes came up and started jumping on me. Someone called the cops, and they arrested me! I mean, there were even kids at the school that watched the fight, and they knew I hadn't started nothing. But I got arrested and charged with fifth-degree assault and damage to property. The damaged property was the kid's coat, which I tore."

Maniac says that he knew he would be at risk in Duluth simply because there were so few black people there.

"Those cops don't see many black kids," he says. "They didn't trust me even before this. I mean, it seemed like every day they were stopping me, asking me what I was doing while I was walking along. One time they even gave me a smoking ticket because I was only seventeen. Just stupid things, just to harass me.

"But that boy, the one who started the whole thing, the one who called me nigger? He got no charges at all. Like I said, some people came forward and told the cops what had really happened, but they didn't listen."

A DIFFERENT KIND OF PRISON

After being convicted of his charges, Maniac was sent to a prison for juvenile offenders in a small town southeast of the city. It was an experience that he says proved to be positive for him.

"It's a prison, yeah, for kids. Everyone seventeen or younger. And they have security there, but there were some freedoms we didn't have at that first jail, the one in the city. Here we had radios in the rooms, and we could play football and basketball and stuff. And there was a game room, with cards and Monopoly and games like that to play.

"The kids there were really different from each other. I mean, other than their ages, they didn't have much in common. Some of us were there for fighting or stealing cars. And there were some kids who had murdered, or raped, or done armed robbery. But everybody was cool; everybody talked to everybody else. The staff was good, too. I suppose there was some racism there somewhere. I mean, it's hard to imagine any place without it. But it wasn't like in the other jail. It didn't show as much, so it was all right."

Maniac spent time in a juvenile prison, where the focus was not punishment, but rather learning to effectively deal with life's problems.

Maniac believes that the prison was good because of its focus. Rather than being primarily a place for punishing bad deeds, it was a training ground for juveniles to go back into the world and accomplish something.

"The idea was to make the place as close to the real world as they could," he explains. "I mean, none of us was going to get out of there and return to a perfectly fair world or one that didn't have any problems. So they help you learn to deal with the problems and the unfairness. They want us to be okay in the real world, not have more problems. I could understand that.

"They liked me there because I was straightforward," he says. "I said what I thought, which used to get me in trouble in other places. Here, if I did something, I'd tell them. If I was planning on doing something, I'd tell them. If I saw somebody do something, and the staff asked me about it, I'd tell them that I didn't have nothing to do with it, and they'd believe me. That by itself was real nice."

The time went by quickly at the juvenile facility, and Maniac found himself enjoying it.

"The days went by real fast," he admits. "You have more things to do, I guess. I mean, in the other jail, you read, eat, read, go to sleep. But at this place there was a school, stuff to do all the time. I learned at that school, too. I got A's and B's. Two C's. Best grades I ever got.

"There were some kids who didn't do so well. They had a hard time with authority. I did, too. I mean, people don't like being told, 'Go to school; now go eat lunch'—stuff like that. It's against their nature. I used to say, 'Hey, my mama can't even tell me what to do, so how the hell do you think I'm letting you do that?' That's the way it was at group home, too.

"But I got by that. Maybe it was that I was older, or maybe it just sunk in finally. Or maybe they said it better at this place. I don't know. But I just started looking at prison in a different way. I looked at it like a job. I figured, if I do good, I get paid. And paid meant getting out, so I worked for that.

"One nice thing is that I had Krista, my girlfriend, come visit me. I'm still going with her. I'd met her once at group home, when they let a bunch of us go to Skateland. She was there, and we got to know each other. So Krista would come to see me in prison every weekend. Her parents like me, too."

Do they call him Maniac? He laughs.

"No, I let them call me Charles," he says. "They're great; they treat me real nice. Her mom even calls me her son."

TERMS OF RELEASE

Nine months after arriving at prison, Maniac was given his release papers. The prison's method for determining whether an inmate should be released is somewhat strange, Maniac says.

"They first of all make you ask your peers, the ones you're serving time with, if they think you're ready to go. They are supposed to say if they feel you are doing better. And the staff, they have to answer the same questions. I don't know about that part, about the peers. It seems kind of silly, even asking them. I mean, I don't know how I'd ever say someone *wasn't* ready to leave. How could I do that?

"But the staff talks about it, too. They talk, they counsel you, everybody has something to say. Then I go to a hearing officer, and he tells me what I've got to do when I get released. At first I tell him whatever I think he needs to hear, yeah. That's how I felt at first, but then, once I got out here, I really did want to do those things that he talked about."

What *did* the hearing officer talk about? Maniac says that the terms of his release are fairly standard.

"I'm supposed to get a job, finish high school. I'm not supposed to hang around with people that are going to get me in trouble, for obvious reasons. And that's about it. I mean, now I'm eighteen, so I don't have a curfew or anything. Just common sense, now."

"I KNOW WHAT I'M DOING"

Today Maniac lives in his grandmother's house, along with his mother and one of his sisters.

"My other sister has her own place. My stepfather's not allowed here; I won't let him be here. They were never married, so he can't say he's coming around to see his wife. My next-oldest brother is fourteen. He's a GD, does his own little thing. He goes to school, looks for a job, runs away from his foster home. I wish my brothers could live here with us, too, but things aren't that way now.

"My mom is off drugs now, and that's good. She went through rehab. She's got no job or anything. She just stays here. I'm hoping she'll be off the drugs for good. My grandma is busy, like she's always been. She gets up early every day and goes out for breakfast with her friends and goes shopping. She'll be back around two o'clock. That's been the way she is since before I was born, I think. She's got a life she likes."

He is interrupted by a chorus of "Hi, Maniac!" from three small children walking by on the sidewalk. He flashes them a big smile and waves. They wave back.

35

"What you kids doing down here? Where's your mom at?"

They assure him that they're doing an errand and that their mother knows where they are. He shakes his head.

"I worry about little kids around here. Those kids like me. They look up to me because I'm not out there all gang-banging and stuff. I help with money sometimes, too. I tell them to go to school. The other day I bought them a club membership. See that building down there, the red brick one? That's a boys and girls club. They got a gym and stuff. I bought the membership so they wouldn't be out here, just . . . . You know what I'm saying? I ain't got a lot of money, but when I do have it, I help out."

A changed person? Maniac says, "Definitely. I've always looked out for little kids. That hasn't changed. I mean, with my little brothers and sisters, that was my job. But the other thing? Yeah. I know what I'm doing. I still have my friends in the gang—guys that are doing the killing and the shooting. But there's me, just trying to go to school and get a job. We're different now, but we're still friends. I ain't going to [put] down nobody for doing what they do. I just tell them, don't bring that around me.

"People might look at me and say, 'He shouldn't be hanging out with that kind of people.' Like maybe I'm too weak to be myself, like they're going to turn me back into a gangbanger the way I was. Well, I think it's none of their business. I'm still straightforward, like in prison. I tell people the truth. And if they don't like it, I guess that's on them."

Martin

"THE TIME THAT WAS WORST [IN
JC] WAS LATE AT NIGHT, WHEN I
COULDN'T SLEEP. I KEPT THINK-
ING ABOUT HOW MAD I WAS THAT
I WAS THERE—NOT JUST THAT I
GOT CAUGHT, BUT THAT I'D DONE
IT IN THE FIRST PLACE. . . . I
WONDERED WHAT THE JUDGE
WOULD SAY. . . . WOULD I GET
SENT SOMEWHERE AWAY FROM
HOME?"

There is a burnt-rubber smell that hangs in the air around the small duplex, a lingering reminder of the busy freeway below. Broken glass lies on the street in front, along with trash from a nearby fast-food restaurant.

Within a little privacy fence is Martin's family's half of the duplex. His father, a Native American with a long ponytail and glasses, sits in the sun. He has almost no expression as he indicates that his son is inside. Beside him sits his younger son, a dimple-faced boy of six or seven. This boy, in sharp contrast to his father, smiles and waves at the visitor.

"I'm Buddy," he says happily. "My brother is inside. He's waiting in there for you."

Martin, sixteen years old, is indeed inside, sitting on a well-used sofa in his living room. Although it is a beautiful July afternoon with plenty of sunshine and a breeze blowing, he is spending the day in this room. In fact, he says, he spends *all* of his days inside, ever since he was released from the juvenile corrections facility downtown. Martin is under house arrest, a prisoner in his own home.

"This Is Just Like Prison"

Martin looks far too young to be a prisoner of any kind. He is wearing cut-off jeans and a T-shirt; a blue baseball hat is jammed tightly onto his head, making it difficult to see his eyes.

"We didn't always live here," he says, with a hint of defensiveness. "This is a crappy neighborhood, and we know it. But we lived up north, in a suburb up there, before we moved here. That neighborhood was a lot nicer. In fact, every place we've lived has been lots nicer than this.

"The one thing about living up there, though, is that there weren't any other people to talk to. I'm Native [American], and that suburb is—well, it's pretty white. No other Natives there, at least none that I ever saw—no kids, anyway. And a lot of the kids didn't have too much in common with me, I guess.

"Here it's pretty loud, with the highway right down below us and everything. It doesn't ever get quiet, even at, like, three in the morning. Always trucks or something. And lots of crime. And the other place where we lived was always quiet. Almost not *enough* going on, you know?"

Martin stops, as if to catch his breath. He adjusts the bill of his cap so that his eyes are more visible.

"Anyway, we live here. My mom and dad and my brothers and me. Right now this is just like prison for me. I've got to wear this thing, see?" He holds up his ankle, where a black box is attached.

"This thing is how they've got me locked up. I mean, I got no locks on the doors or nothing. I just wear this. It looks like a big pager, I think, and it stays on with this band, kind of like a watch. The other part of it is plugged into the wall over there in the kitchen. It's kind of like a telephone jack, and it has lights on it. It goes off, sends off some kind of alarm, if I go too far away from the plug-in part. I'm not sure of the range, but I don't really want to test it to find out."

Until now there has been the sound of dishes being washed in the kitchen, but as Martin finishes talking, the noise stops. A woman moves haltingly into the living room. Although she is young, the shoulder harness and neck brace she wears restrain her movements, making her seem closer to seventy than thirty-five.

"You should say you are Ojibwa, not just Native," she corrects her son. She ignores the visitor at first. "And say, 'the Red Lake branch,' too, to be more specific."

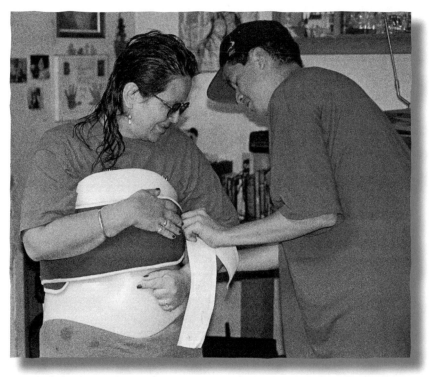

Martin helps his mother with her brace, which she has worn since she fell from a loft and broke her back and shoulder. He lives under house arrest with her, his father, and his younger brothers.

"Yeah," says Martin obediently. "The Red Lake branch. We're registered at the res [reservation]. We've been up there."

His mother smiles slightly and walks slowly outside, closing the door behind her.

"That's my mom," says Martin with concern in his voice. "She's in pretty bad shape, I guess you could say. See that bandage and everything around her chest? She got hurt—fell out of the loft up there. She broke her spinal cord, her back, and her shoulder in three places. The way it happened was, it was the middle of the night, and she just rolled over and fell. She pinched some kind of nerve in her brain, too, so she started having seizures, like fits. She turned blue and everything.

"My dad has worked as a nursing assistant in the ER, so he knew it was real serious. He helped her, kept her quiet, and called 911. She's in bad shape, but I think she's going to be okay. She's got to take some medicine to keep the seizures from coming back, but the doctors said in three months she'll get better."

Landlord and Employment Problems

Martin says he feels that the stress of his arrest has not helped his mother feel any better. He wishes it all could be over with so that things could get back to normal.

"But the thing is, I don't think things could be normal until my dad gets a job again," he says. "He doesn't work now. He's pretty much always home now. Sometimes he goes off to a job interview. I think he and my mom were talking about sometime next week he might go see a vocational counselor. That's someone who can help him get lined up with a job or figure out what kind of training he needs, or whatever.

"He used to be a nursing assistant, like I said before. My mom worked, too. She was basically taking care of me and my brothers during the day, and later when my dad came home from the ER, she would go off to her job. She worked at a hospital, too, as a nurse. They got paid pretty good, too. That's back when we lived in that one suburb."

Exactly why his father is now unemployed is a subject that Martin is uncomfortable talking about. He does say, however, that it was not that his father got laid off or fired.

"It's just that there was some business going on with where we lived," he says, shrugging. "We had this nice old house, a really big one. Lots of rooms for all of us. I'm the oldest of the four boys; my littlest brother is six, so it was cool that we had our own rooms. Not like we are living now.

"We had problems with the landlord in our house. She didn't like our loud music, was the main thing, I guess. She kicked us out and pulled some stupid tricks, like not letting us get our stuff out of the house. We tried. We went back, but we couldn't get our furniture, some clothes, lots of stuff. And she didn't send no form, like you're supposed to do, saying a tenant is kicked out. So by law, she didn't do things right.

"So anyway, with that stuff happening, it was hard for my dad to keep the job in the ER, the one that paid so good. So we went looking—actually my parents went looking—closer to the city for a place for us to live. This is all we could afford, for right now. And so when we moved here, that's when the trouble started. My trouble, anyway."

Martin says that the biggest drawback of the duplex they rented was the neighborhood.

Times have been difficult for Martin's family since his father, who worked as a nursing assistant, became unemployed.

"I started hanging around with a whole different group of people," he explains. "And I don't mean to be blaming my troubles on them, but I did get into some bad stuff. I think it was a combination of things: me being too weak to say no to some stuff and maybe not being used to hanging around like that. I was just unaccustomed to it, really.

"See, back where I lived before, the kids were really snotty. A lot of them were. Especially about school things. I was a good student back then, especially in eighth grade. I made the honor roll, and I had to work hard for it. I'm smart, I think, but I have to study hard to make A's and B's.

"But instead of getting support for being smart, lots of kids gave me a hard time. It got really bad when one trimester I was the only eighth grader to get on the honor roll. My parents were real proud. I was, too, but it wasn't worth all the crap I got at school. It's like all of a sudden no one was my friend."

The friends he met when he moved to the city were not students at all, says Martin. They were more interested in hanging out and getting in trouble. And to be included, Martin went right along with them.

"I started really screwing up, really bad," he admits. "I didn't go to school much, and when I did I didn't study. Didn't do much of anything, really. What I liked to do was hang out at the park with my new friends. They weren't like the kids in the suburbs: They were Native; some were black. I even got into a gang."

LITTLE BOY BLUE

Martin joined the Gangster Disciples gang when he was fifteen. He learned quickly that even though he was not necessarily looking for trouble, he began finding it.

"It got hard sometimes," he says. "I don't think we planned to do stuff we did. But all the time you're hanging around, just talking and passing the time. And what happens? Some guy walks through your neighborhood, and then there's words back and forth, back and forth. And all of a sudden it's, like, people are fighting. How did it happen? Who knows?

"We didn't usually fight the Crips. We're cool with them. I mean, the GD Folk up here in this city came about because of the Crips. We're like their cousins. So not too much bad stuff going down with the Crips. The fighting itself wasn't a problem for me. I can fight okay. I can take a punch, too. I got jumped in [initiated, usually violently] with the GDs—ten or twelve of those guys punching you for about six minutes. That was hard, but I did it. And you can't fight back, or they'll really beat the crap out of you. So you take it, walking straight through the line of them, letting them punch you.

"They're not allowed to hit you in the nose or the eyes. Head shots aren't really allowed at all, but mouth shots are okay." He winces, remembering. "I felt like my jaw was out of place for a few weeks afterwards. When it was happening, I guess it passed through my mind, What are you doing, Martin? Why are you letting these guys beat you up? But when it was done, and I was in, I was a BG, a baby gangster. They called me Little Boy Blue; that was my nickname."

Martin stands next to the box that detects if he goes out of range. He says his problems began with some new friends who were more interested in hanging out and getting into trouble than attending school.

Martin says his parents did not know about his gang affiliation, nor would they have understood if they had known. "They are real nice people," he says loyally. "I mean, I can't say my parents are bad, like some of those guys do. Some of them don't have fathers, or their mothers are on crack or are drunks, or whatever. My parents are cool. I mean, I don't always get along with them, but we do okay.

"And I can't complain about my childhood being unhappy either," he says. "I had a real nice childhood. I remember doing a lot of stuff with my parents and my baby brothers. We went up to the res a couple of times, had fun together. I mean, it wasn't like we didn't have fights sometimes, but I liked being a kid in this family."

Martin says his parents caught him smoking marijuana with some friends and tried to punish him—but to no avail.

"My parents didn't know," he says. "They didn't know how bad I was doing until this last crime. I mean, when they caught us smoking out on the side of the house, they were real mad. I got

Unlike many gang members, Martin's childhood was relatively happy and he got along with his parents. He was attracted by the gang lifestyle, however, and at fifteen was jumped in to the Gangster Disciples.

yelled at. They were angry, probably angrier than they'd ever been. I had to go to my room, and I got grounded for a couple of days. But I kept on sneaking out."

He got caught skipping school, he says, but even though his parents scolded him and told him he had to go to school each day, he found spending time with his friends much more attractive.

"I'd get kicked out of school and then I'd get enrolled in another one," he says, frowning. "I met new people there, started hanging around with them. We hung out, smoked some weed, and it would start all over again. I mean it, I was bad then. I'm not a bad person now, I mean that. But then, I didn't care."

BEING BAD

With these new friends in the city, Martin says that he tried out a lot of new behaviors—things he had never done, or even thought about, before.

"I was messing with marijuana, like I said," he says. "I broke into cars, I drank. I sold some dope here and there, some crack. That was the gang thing, for the leader of the gang. See, he talked to a bunch of us, told us we could turn a real profit on it if we gave it a chance. So I did it. It wasn't too hard, but a little stressful, I will admit.

"You have to keep it in little plastic bags in your mouth. That way, if the police come up to you, you can swallow it. If it's, like, in your pockets or your sock or something, they can catch you with it before you have a chance to throw it. So you store the little bag of crack under your tongue. It feels weird at first, but you get used to it after about an hour."

What happens to the merchandise if he is forced to swallow it? Is it simply a case of profits lost? Martin laughs.

"It shits out," he explains. "That's how they do it in prison, when they bring it in cell blocks, how the drugs get passed from person to person in the big prisons. I've heard that from guys who have been there. They swallow the stuff, and later, when it comes out, they've got their drugs. That's dangerous, see, because if the bag is faulty, or your stomach has lots of acid, then the plastic can be eaten away, and you could die real easy. That's happened to people. Anyway, that's how I avoided getting caught. And I never did."

The crime that he found most daring, he says, was robbing people on the street. It was definitely something he had never envisioned himself doing.

"I didn't like it," he says flatly. "I felt like I had to be looking around constantly. Too stressful. And that was with a lot of my gang friends with me. I couldn't ever have done that on my own! But it was like a lot of other stuff: You'd be sitting around with other people and talking, and you try out things you never did before. It's what they did, that's all.

"Anyway, how it happened, was one night we were just hanging around, and some young guy comes walking down the street. He was young, yeah—midtwenties, I'd say. Black, a different set [gang] than us, he had his hat cocked off to the left. Maybe a Vice Lord. We didn't get along too good with them.

"So he's coming, and we pulled out our guns, told him to give up the money. We took his money, his watch and gold rings, stuff like that. He wasn't too afraid, either. I'll always remember that. It didn't seem like he was surprised or worried. That was strange, I think. I'd have been real scared."

Martin says that after that he became a lot braver about doing crimes.

ROBBING HOUSES

"It was, like, I got more and more daring," he says. "I got caught up in it, you know? I started doing more cars, and then I tried robbing houses. The last time I did it, it was with my cousin, Tony. I got caught, though, and that's the reason I'm here, with this thing on my ankle."

His cousin was a little more experienced than he was, so Martin let Tony choose the house they would rob.

"He knew how to pick out the ones that we'd have the least amount of trouble with," says Martin. "He could spot empty ones real good. See, you look for a place with a lot of mail in the mailbox. That tips you off that the people are on vacation or something, maybe away for the weekend. And you don't want no dogs or little signs that said they were signed up with some security company.

"So this house was over in St. Paul. It wasn't in a rich neighborhood, but not in a poor one, either. Just sort of in the middle. The blinds were shut, and it had that look to it. So we knocked on the door. It was in the morning, and we just wanted to make sure. If someone had come to the door, we'd have just come up with some excuse or other, I guess. I think Tony would have known what to say."

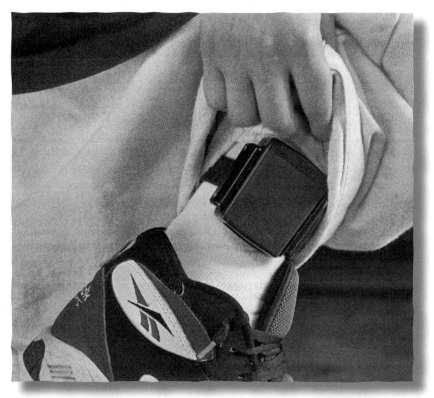

Martin lifts his pants leg to reveal his monitor, the device that allows the police to keep track of him.

They knew they wouldn't waste time trying to get in by picking a lock or prying open a window.

"The way we'd do it was strictly breaking in," he says. "We'd kick in a door, break a window. Nothing very fancy. We had backpacks with us to put in the stuff we wanted. We were looking for leather jackets, gold, stuff like that. Anything we found, I guess. My cousin knew people we could dump the stuff with, on the street, to get paid for it."

CAUGHT IN THE ACT

Martin says that once they had entered the house, he began to get excited. "It's like an adrenaline rush," he admits. "It feels really strange, really powerful. You're in someone's house, and only you know that. You keep thinking, Will I get caught? What's that noise? You listen really hard, and everything seems to be really clear, and you are just thinking, thinking. I don't know, it's like the time goes really slowly. Once you come out of the house . . . you

Martin and his cousin were caught by the police after robbing a house. During the robbery, Martin says he experienced an adrenaline rush.

haven't been in there more than a couple of minutes, but it seems like hours.

"Me and Tony had been in the house, looking through the stuff in there, and we'd found a lot of things. I had a camcorder, leather jackets, some fourteen karat gold rings, earrings, watches, stuff like that. We had stuffed most of it in backpacks, and we just walked outside.

"But the first thing we saw was a cop car, just creeping toward the house. I guess some ladies had seen us breaking in and called 911. The cops didn't have their lights or siren on, just creeping, like I said. We were pretty easy to see, since it was light. There wasn't anywhere we could just run to that would be a hiding place. I wanted to run, but Tony didn't. I didn't want to leave him there while I ran, but I wish we could have. I mean, that was my first instinct, you know, just get out of there fast."

Martin says that he and Tony began walking back toward the house, as though they had not been there. They hoped that if they could trick the police, they would be able to get away.

"We were trying to look innocent." He smiles. "It wasn't a very good plan, or maybe we just didn't do it right. But the cops jumped out and yelled for us to get on the ground, which we did. The one cop started questioning us, asking us did we steal a car. We hadn't done that, though; we'd taken the bus to this house."

The police drove Martin and his cousin to the precinct station, where they were fingerprinted, photographed, and locked up.

PARENTAL SUPPORT

"We were allowed to call home, so I did," says Martin. "I was more scared about talking to my parents than anything else. My dad was really surprised at what I had done, and he said, 'Well, you know, Son, we are really sorry that you've done this, but we know things will work out for you.'

"They were mostly worried about how I'd be certified, you know? Certified means, do you stand trial as an adult or as a minor? See, they have this graph, kind of a chart, that the judges or whatever use to figure out how someone should be certified. Like, how many prior arrests, or things like that. And how you get certified decides where you get locked up. If you get certified as an adult, then you go to a regular prison, with adult prisoners. A kid goes to juvenile institution, which is run different.

"My cousin, Tony, is only a month older than me, but because of what he'd done before—different crimes and whatever—he had to get certified as an adult. This was bad for him, because he had to do real prison time, and it would be on his record forever. But me, I hadn't done much stuff before, so I was still considered a minor, which was lucky for me."

Martin says that he was grateful that his parents were as forgiving as they were toward him.

"I was really worried before talking to them, because I didn't know what they'd say," he says. "But they were always by me, always by my side. My mom said she thought it was important for them to treat me with respect, because even though I'd done bad stuff, I was a young man. I mean, they treated me with respect because I am their son and they love me. After that, man, I knew that anything I did . . . I never had to be worried about coming to them. That was a relief.

"But it wasn't like they were easy on me, or anything. They made it real clear that I should have thought more before I got into the situation and that they were real disappointed in me. And they knew I was mad at myself, which I really was. I didn't blame my cousin. I blamed myself. It was a stupid thing to do, and we all knew that.

"My cousin, in a way I feel sorry for him. His mom is handicapped, I guess you could say. She's got a brace on her leg, and she can't get after Tony as much as she should. She just can't do nothing about it, no matter what he does and no matter how mad she gets at him. And he never knew his dad, so there's only one parent for him. So he gets away with a lot more, and that's bad for him."

In JC

Martin stayed in the juvenile corrections facility, known as JC, while waiting for his court date. His father and mother did not come to see him, although they talked to him by telephone.

"I stayed at JC all that time, waiting," he remembers. "It's not a great place to be for more than a night or two. I'd been there before, once when I was arrested for auto theft. And, man, the first time, it's pretty scary going in there. You don't know who you can

Martin sits on the couch with his younger brother. Martin is grateful for the love and support his parents have given him following his arrest.

talk to, you don't know what's going to happen. You don't know anything.

"This time I knew that some of the people would be mean and others would be scary. It's just the way it is. Some of the guards you can get to know, and you try to get along with them. It's a busy place, lots of noise, lots of business happening all the time. One thing I remember thinking my first time there is that no one seems to be worrying about you, how you're feeling. Just you. And since Tony had been shipped off to a different facility, one for older people, we didn't have each other to talk to.

"There are a lot of sounds, too. People are yelling, kids are swearing—mad that they're there. No one wants to be told what to do, and lots of the kids in there are making sure the guards know that. It just felt like there was never any time when it was quiet or peaceful. But that was just for a day, that first time, and then I was released back home. This time, I was in for a little longer time.

"And it smelled like vinegar," he says. "I think that's because they use vinegar to clean with or something. Anyway, it was a really bad smell. You get your own room sometimes, but if they get really crowded, which it does sometimes, you got to get doubled up. One of the guards I talked to told me that there were about 140 kids there the last time I was there. In the year 2000, he says, they might be looking at over 200 kids at one time! All under seventeen, all mad because they're there. Lots of them gang kids, too, so they're pretty scary sometimes."

ALONE WITH HIS THOUGHTS

For Martin one of the worst things about being at JC was the boredom. "It's hard to describe how boring it is," he says. "You're locked in your room most of the time. You read books and magazines. You watch television, and you eat. The food isn't terrible; it's not home cooking or anything, but it's better than you might think.

"The time that was the worst was late at night, when I couldn't sleep. I kept thinking about how mad I was that I was there—not just that I got caught, but that I'd done it in the first place. And I worried about how things were going to turn out. I wondered what the judge would say. I mean, I pleaded guilty, but who knows? Would I get sent somewhere away from home? Would I get taken away from my family? And at night that kind of stuff seems a lot more real. There's nothing to distract you from thinking negative thoughts like that."

"I Made a Commitment"

Martin was in JC for two weeks until his court date. By the end of that two-week period, he had made an important decision.

"I made a commitment—to myself and my parents," he says earnestly. "My commitment was that I was never going to mess up like this again. I was going to put that bad stuff behind me, and I was determined that I wasn't going to have no adult record. There was nothing I could do about my juvenile record, but I *could* make sure it never transferred over to my adult life, you know?

"During the two weeks I was there, I saw my counselor advocate. He was working hard to get me released; he told the court that I was a good kid. And I am."

Martin says the last three words forcefully.

"He told me that JC wasn't built for kids to stay in a long time," he says. "Most of the time kids are there for a weekend, or even overnight. The longest I ever heard anybody staying there is three months. That's pretty hard to imagine—man! Usually, though, they try to get you into some permanent place as soon as possible.

"So my counselor advocate came in and I made a commitment to him, too. I told him he could believe me when I told him I wasn't going to do that shit anymore. I wouldn't mess up ever again, I said. I didn't want to let him down, and he really did think I'm a good kid. He believed me, too. He told me he didn't want to mess up his reputation by standing behind some bad kid. That would show people he was a bad judge of character, he said."

Martin's counselor advocate was successful in getting his client sent home, to be imprisoned under house arrest until the final court hearing would determine his punishment.

"So they came to my house and put me into this thing," he says, motioning toward the monitor. "I hate it, yeah. Like I said before, it's always with me. It's the first thing I think about in the morning and the last thing I think about at night. I feel it all the time because it's bulky and heavy. I've got to shower with it, sleep with it.

"It hasn't ever gone off, not since I've had it on. If it went off, I probably wouldn't hear it, anyway. I think the alarm would only go off downtown, and then the cops would come and see what happened. I'm not allowed outside. That much I know. And that's the hardest part. I mean, I get up and I look out the window and see people walking around outside. The weather's nice, the sun is shining. And it's like teasing, man. It is. It's like teasing you, being so close to outside.

After two weeks in jail, Martin had made up his mind to put the past behind him and focus on his future: "I made a commitment—to myself and my parents. . . . I was never going to mess up like this again."

"At least when you're in JC, you know you're nowhere near outside. No way you're going to breathe outside air or see the sunshine, you know? You're locked up, there. Here, I see everything. I watch the cars, the people. I see the squirrels and the dogs and cats. I feel like I'm less free than a dog or a cat. I got less to do, that's for sure.

"I've been here inside, home from JC, for two months. That's not too long, I know," he says, shaking his head. "But really, it feels like two years to me. Maybe if it was winter now, it wouldn't be so bad, I don't know. It's just so hard. The only time I've been out of the house in the last two months is when I had to go to the Indian Health Board and get my physical. We had to call up to tell the people monitoring this thing that I'd be disconnected for a while. We got permission. But then, right back on it."

POSITIVE ATTITUDE

It is easy to believe Martin when he claims that he is done with crime forever. Just thinking about an adult prison, he says, gives him nightmares.

"Being with a bunch of adults and the stories you hear about young guys being older guys' boyfriends . . . God, I'd hate that," he says with a shudder. "Man, I know I won't ever get certified. I'll be good now, and then when I'm eighteen, they'll erase my record, so I don't have my past mistakes hanging over me.

"I know it will be hard—it's not like I live in some perfect world around here," he says. "I mean, I'll still want to see my old friends, hang out. I'm still a GD, but I ain't going to be getting into stuff like they do. If they start talking about doing some robbery, I'm not included. I mean, they wouldn't be talking about robbing no house, but if they were talking about robbing a person in the street, they'd know I wouldn't.

"If they said something about some crime, I'd be, like, 'Nope.' That would be that, too. Whatever you hear about people in gangs forcing each other to do stuff is wrong. At least, it doesn't apply to my friends. Any pressure is just peer pressure or something, I don't know. It's not that anybody's making you do stuff.

"Those guys are still my friends, I know that. They'll be loyal to me. They know I'm eager to be good, so they'll help me lay low. They aren't about trying to get me in more trouble, get me sent away or certified. So I'm not worried about that, not really."

Martin looks outside, where he is not allowed to go under house arrest. He says it is very difficult to be near the fresh air and sunshine and not be able to step out the door.

For the time being, Martin says, he is just eager to be done with his time under house arrest.

"I've read a lot of books," he says. "I've always liked to read, so that isn't too bad, I guess. Stephen King books are my favorite, and we got a couple of those around here. And I watch television, but it gets on my nerves sometimes."

If he wanted to have his friends come in, if his parents weren't home, could he? How could his ankle bracelet alert police?

"It couldn't," he says simply. "I mean, the deal is that nobody's supposed to visit. You're okay, but only because the judge and whatever said it was okay. But no one else is supposed to visit me. That's the point, to keep me away from outside influences, to make sure I don't mess up. But like you say, it's possible to see people if I was determined to do that. If I was a guy who wanted to get in more trouble, I could. I'd just wait until my mom and dad weren't home, and call people and tell them to come over.

"The juvenile court told me the terms of this house arrest, and if they come over and I'm messing up, I'm in trouble, big-time. It's up to me. I mean, they can come for as many unscheduled visits as they want. It's just the risk. And I'm not interested in taking that risk."

The telephone, says Martin, has been an inconvenience ever since his arrest. Although he is allowed to talk on the phone, there is an electronic attachment on it now that makes long conversations impossible.

"They want the phone clear all the time so when they call in from downtown once in a while, they can reach you," he explains. "So there's this weird noise that starts, that, like, scrambles the sound on the phone. You can't really hear what the other person is saying. I just yell, 'Call me back!' when that happens. It goes off after about two minutes, I guess. I think it's probably more of a nuisance for my parents."

THINKING AHEAD

Martin knows that once his house arrest is done, he'll be placed in a group home of some sort, at least temporarily.

"I'm pretty sure I'm going up north, to a group home there," he says. "I hear it's a pretty good program, too. The whole idea for juvenile offenders isn't just to punish kids, but to make sure they have a chance to work out the stuff that made them do the crimes in the first place. My lawyer thought I could do a pretty good job in a program like that one.

"I know they got counselors there, and classrooms so you don't get behind on your schoolwork. Maybe I'll be there three months or so. And then, I guess I come back here. I'm not sure, because my mom and I have been talking about some options.

"See, I sometimes think I'd like to get away from here a little while. I know what I said about my friends in the gang, but I still think it would be nice to move somewhere I don't know so many people. You know what I mean? So people wouldn't always be talking to you about stuff you really don't want to do—just kind of be more on my own.

"So my mom said that maybe I could go live with my aunt and cousins on the other side of town after I get back from my program up north. Or even go up north to live for a while with another aunt. See, we got relatives in nicer places, and maybe that would be good. I know that gangs are in every place, even up north. But starting over, I could just not get real involved, not get in. It would be easier to avoid situations up there, you know? It's hard to explain. I just feel like I know too much about how things go on around here."

Martin shrugs his shoulders. "I don't know what will happen. Maybe I'll be fine, coming back here. I'd get back into school, I know that. I've been going to an alternative school. I did up until I got into trouble, anyway. My parents wanted me to go to this other school; it's more for Native kids. They think it's important for me to be around more kids from my own culture, my own heritage.

"So maybe I'll do that. Or maybe I'll get into the Job Corps here. They got programs just like a regular school, only you take classes in certain jobs, too. That way you're all ready to be hired when

Martin demonstrates his gang sign. Although he intends to continue his friendships with other gang members, he wants nothing to do with crime in the future, and instead will focus on education and job skills.

you finish, and you know all the skills. I think about construction, sometimes. Maybe I'd be good at that."

Martin says that one of the reasons he'd want to stay closer to home is to make sure his younger brothers don't fall into the same traps that he has.

"I got three little brothers," he says. "One of them is just a couple of years younger than me—fourteen now. I worry about him. He's in his own little land right now. I don't like to think about him doing what I did—hanging in the park with his friends, getting into stuff. But I don't know. I don't feel comfortable talking to them about being under house arrest. I feel kind of embarrassed about it, especially with my little brothers. It's, like, I'm always here, and that kind of reminds them that I couldn't leave if I wanted to.

"I'd tell them to stay clear of that stuff, though, if they asked me," he says. "I'd say, 'Don't do the stuff I've done, because you pay for it. You're going to think about it all your life, and it comes down on you. You may not think it will, but it will.'

"It's no good talking about consciences. Someone asked me if my conscience was bothering me when I was robbing that house or robbing that dude in the park. It wasn't. Maybe that means I was really bad, but all I was thinking about was how good it would be to get that money, to find jewelry or a leather coat. I wasn't thinking about right and wrong."

Martin takes his hat off and runs his hands through his hair.

"But that doesn't mean I don't think about it now. I mean, I think about it all the time. Sometimes I forget for a while, if I'm watching television or something. And then I'll move, and I'll feel [the monitor] there. And then I think about the crime again, and how I wish I hadn't done that.

"Sometimes I try to concentrate on the good things that happen. Like, the perfect day for me: sleeping late, kicking back and listening to music, and playing baseball with some friends. That would be fun. Maybe I'll do that stuff again sometime."

Kara

"I'VE PROBABLY BEEN IN MORE
JAILS, PRISONS, REHAB CENTERS,
HOSPITALS, FOSTER HOMES, AND
GROUP HOMES IN THIS STATE
THAN ANYONE I KNOW. I'VE SEEN
THEM ALL, AND I'LL TELL YOU, I'M
GLAD I'M FREE AT HOME NOW."

"If you can't find out what you need about lockups for teenagers by talking to me, then you just aren't listening," says Kara with a laugh. "I've probably been in more jails, prisons, rehab centers, hospitals, foster homes, and group homes in this state than anyone I know. I've seen them all, and I'll tell you, I'm glad I'm free at home now."

She pauses, looking down at the bulky electronic monitor strapped to her ankle.

"Actually I'm not really free—at least not until day after tomorrow. But it's good to be home, anyway. And if you only knew how strange it is to be saying *that*! I never thought I would hear myself say those words, not ever!"

Kara is a pretty, petite Korean girl of seventeen. She is wearing a lot of dark makeup and a tight top and jean shorts. She is sitting in her mother's apartment in a suburb west of the city. Her mother is at work now. Her older sister is up north working at a resort. Kara has the place to herself this afternoon, but she doesn't mind.

"I've never had too much of a problem being alone," she says in an easy, self-possessed voice. "I spent a lot of time that way when I was younger. I never fit in, see. I was always different—different from others in my family, different from kids at school, different from anyone I ever saw in the community.

"I've pretty much always lived here, and it is *really* white. I was adopted by my mom and dad when I was eight months old, so I don't remember any other home than this. My dad works for the county, dealing with some kind of adult mental health or something. I don't really know the details of what he does, since we don't talk much. My parents are divorced, see, since I was two or three years old."

BEING DIFFERENT

"For most of my life I didn't know much about the details of my life back in Korea," she says. "But just recently I have been reading about it, the adoption records and everything. I guess my birth mother couldn't take care of me; my birth father had split. So she took me some place to give me up. I know that in Korea it's a lot tougher than here to be a single mother."

Kara says that her life as an adopted Korean girl has not been easy at all. "I've always felt really different," she says. "I mean, I was different because I was adopted, and I think there were some jealousy issues with my older sister. I mean, both of us had issues. She was jealous of me because I was this new baby in the house, and I was jealous of her as time went on because she was always so good, so smart, so everything.

"And when I got to school, I was the only Korean kid. I remember thinking, man, everybody but me in this world is white. There were lots of comments at school. Kids called me slant eyes and sang little songs about Chinese people."

Did it hurt her feelings? She shrugs.

"At first, yeah. When I was little the snide comments hurt. I mean, everyone wants to fit in, to be like everyone else, when you're young, right? But after a while, I guess I convinced myself that if they were teasing me, they just weren't worth my time. And when I got older, there were more races out there, too. But in grade school it was, like, me against the world."

As she is talking, Kara seems distracted by her ankle monitor. With a sigh of exasperation, she yanks at it, rotating it so that the bulky monitor is on the inside of her ankle.

"This is *so* annoying," she says. "I can't forget about it, even for a minute. I have really bony ankles, and it's always hitting the bone. I'm glad I only have to wear this for a couple more days. I don't really think of myself as a bad kid at all. I mean, there are a lot of kids that wear these things, and they've done really bad crimes. I don't think I've really done anything that bad, just mostly running [away]. And I've done a lot of that, I admit.

"Anyway, where was I? Oh, my childhood. Well, my parents got divorced, like I said. And afterwards, my mom remarried, and I got a stepbrother. But they didn't stay married long, so it was just the three of us after a while—my mom, my sister, and me. My mom is single now. I don't think she's looking to get married again.

"So the trouble for me started when I was twelve. I guess it had been building up before that, but it was then that I started really running away a lot. See, everything just escalated with my mom and me. We'd fight over everything: school, how I dressed, who I hung out with, what time I had to come in—everything.

"When I'd run, I'd go to a friend's house, usually this one girl-friend. She was kind of on her own, she and her brother. Her mom had a boyfriend, so she was always over at his house. I guess my friend and her brother were pretty much raising themselves. There were always kids over there, just hanging out."

As an adopted Korean in a white family, Kara felt different from other people. She was the only Korean student in her school, and endured the taunts of other children. By age twelve, she was fighting with her mother and began running away.

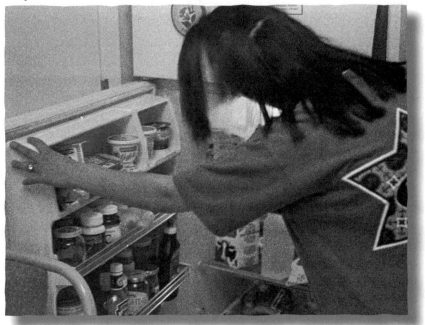

"KIDS ARE SHALLOW"

Kara says that her mother was more interested in her fitting in than she was, although she repeats that she might have wanted to get along when she was younger. She just lost interest after a while, she says.

"I got teased about my clothes, teased about my hair. I don't know. It wasn't how the cheerleaders were, so they thought it was weird. The cliques bothered me at first; they were so smug about everything. But I know the stuff they thought was so important really wasn't.

"Kids are shallow," she says simply. "They feel superior because they have money or because their parents are together—all sorts of reasons. But I couldn't help what my situation was. I admit that, now, looking back, I could have done some things differently at school. I could have given some of the kids more of a chance. I mean, once I started being different, I purposely went way out of my way being *really* different. So maybe I alienated people."

The circle of friends that she did have was unacceptable to her mother, Kara states flatly.

"They weren't all that good, I know that," she says. "They were fighters, a lot of tough kids. They smoked, they drank, all kinds of stuff my mom didn't like. See, I had an older cousin, Paul. He went to the high school, and he had friends whose brothers and sisters went to the middle school where I was. He told those kids to watch over me, make sure I didn't get picked on.

"So they did." She laughs. "I mean, I never had to fight my own battles. These guys looked out for me, yeah. I knew that they weren't all that good, though. But my mom making an issue of it made me defend them, I guess. I mean, she'd tell me not to hang out with them or that they were trashy, and I'd get mad and defend them.

"The way me and my mom would fight made me feel bad afterwards. I talked back to her, and sometimes it got physical. Like one time, she told the cops I'd hit her with the phone, even though I hadn't meant to. She tried to grab the phone and I tried to pull it back, and when she yanked on it, it went too far and hit her. But like I said, I always felt bad after a fight.

"I don't think she had a clue how to raise me. And I don't blame her for that. I don't think she could have done any different. I acted out, I rebelled. I don't resent anything she did, because I was the problem. I mean, she was my mom. She brought me up, she was there for me. I think my sister was so easy to raise that my mom couldn't deal with having a problem kid, that's all."

"I JUST WASN'T SMART"

Things got worse and worse, from the summer after sixth grade into her seventh-grade year.

"I was hanging around my friend and her brother and all their friends," she says. "I was running away all the time. I'm sure my mom knew where I was, or at least she had strong suspicions. I'd call her every few days just to let her know I was safe. I didn't say where I was, but she knew I went over there a lot anyway. It made sense that it would be the first place I'd run to, I guess.

"When I was there one time, the police came to the door. I'm sure my mom had told them I had run and that they could find me there. But my friends were really loyal. They wouldn't let the police in the door! They just asked, 'Do you have a warrant?' The police didn't, so they went away."

Kara's time away from home was not spent either wisely or productively, she admits as she looks back.

"I mean, with all those kids around, we just didn't have rules. We sure didn't make any up, and my friend's mother wasn't around. We'd cruise around with some older kids, drink, smoke, skip school. I admit I abused alcohol then, but I wasn't an alcoholic. I was a social drinker, but I did get drunk—to the point where I lost my virginity with some older guy when I was twelve. Too much to drink, just riding around in cars. I just wasn't smart, I guess. I mean, I'd come home after a while, thinking I really wanted to be home. But then something would happen, and I'd be gone again."

At the end of her patience, Kara's mother brought her daughter to a temporary shelter for troubled and runaway teens in the city. "She couldn't handle me any more," says Kara. "She didn't trust me, and she felt like I wasn't getting any better, no matter what I'd promise. So she took me there. And from there it was decided that I was going to live with my dad.

"It definitely wasn't my idea; it was just sort of thrown on me. I had been at the shelter for about two weeks. It was sort of fun. We had field trips, things to do. It was summer, so there wasn't school going on. And I had a counselor who was pretty nice. Anyway, at

Kara's mother could no longer tolerate her running away, drinking, and skipping school, and put Kara in a shelter. Instead of returning to her mother's home, however, Kara was sent to live with her father.

my release session I walked into the room, and there was my mom, my dad, my stepmother, and the counselor.

"We talked for a little while, just about different ways of arguing and about not letting things escalate to major wars. And then, all of a sudden, my mom got up and left the room. Like, it was all planned out beforehand. Like, they all knew, but I didn't. And then my dad says, 'Get your stuff, you're going home with us.'

"I threw a fit. I went so crazy! I started screaming and calling the counselor all these names. I destroyed the spider plant on his desk—just tore it up. My dad and stepmother, I remember, were just standing way in the corner, trying to stay out of my way."

Kara says she knows how ironic it sounds, her being angry because she couldn't return to her mother's house. "Since I ran from there all the time, I guess maybe it is ironic," she says. "But even though I always argued with my mom, she was my mom, you know? And I didn't want her to leave or have to go with my dad. I definitely did not want to go with him."

"There Was a Lot of Abuse There"

Kara's reluctance to move in with her father and his wife was based on a long-standing fear of his temper, a fear, she says, that was grounded in fact.

"He hit me, even when I was really little," she says. "I had to visit him on weekends and holidays sometimes, and I always hated it. There was a lot of abuse there. I remember one time, when I was three, I was riding in his car, and I had to sit in the front seat. The only place I could fit was sort of straddling the gear shift. Anyway, it was real uncomfortable, and when I tried to cross my legs, I knocked the gear shift out of gear. He was so mad at me he backhanded me, really hard. And he never, ever apologized. I was so little, and he didn't even care that he'd hurt me.

"Well, that kind of started up for real once I moved in with him. It hadn't been all the time before, but it started being real regular. If I was late coming home or if he'd had a bad day, he'd come storming into my room and let loose on me, just hitting me. Or if he couldn't find the cordless phone, he'd come into my room and punch me, yell at me.

"He had been in the Vietnam War, like a self-defense instructor, so he was really strong," she says. "He didn't use karate on me or anything, but he'd grab me hard and not let go. He'd grab me by my arms and just shake me, throw me up against the wall."

Did her stepmother step in or try to help? Kara rolls her eyes. "Right," she says sarcastically. "She'd just sit downstairs in front of the television, reading a magazine or something. I don't know if she knew what was going on, and if she did, she sure never said anything. It was a family secret, his being scary. I mean, I don't know if they knew how much he hit me, but they sure knew he yelled a lot. Everyone was afraid of him; he's intimidating."

Nowhere to Go

Kara thought a lot about leaving, but she didn't know many people she could stay with in the community where her father lived. She did find that it helped just staying away from home as much as she could during the evening.

"I had two close friends that I told, but I told them not to tell," she says. "It's hard to explain. I didn't know where I'd get sent if I reported him. I mean, maybe it would be worse than his house. I'd heard rumors about group homes and jails and everything. So when teachers would ask me about a bruise on my arm or something, I'd just make up some excuse. I figured maybe I'd be worse off in one of those other places, so I'd just keep my mouth shut.

"I finally *did* run after I spent Thanksgiving with my mom at her house," she says. "I had been trying to tell my mom about it . . . I just got brave and told her. But she didn't believe me. And thinking back, why should she? I had no bruises then, and I'd been lying to her so much, she probably figured I was lying again. So she just gave me a look and didn't say anything.

"So I ran from her house and decided I'd never go back to my father's, not ever. I went to a friend's, but an ex-boyfriend was there, and he secretly called the police and told them where I was. I was so mad. I thought, man, he's got a lot of nerve turning me in. So the police came and took me out of my friend's house, but not without a fight. I was yelling, kicking, swearing. They heard me say the word *kill* and they took me to a hospital for a mental evaluation. They thought I was saying I was going to kill myself. Really, I was saying I wanted to kill them!"

HOSPITALS, FOSTER HOMES, A SHELTER, AND MORE RUNNING

After it was determined she was definitely not suicidal, Kara was moved to another hospital to be evaluated.

"They knew I had been abused," she says, "and it wasn't an issue about believing me. It was their job to believe me; that's what they were there for. I had social workers, people who talked to me. My mom came out for sessions, too. She felt bad that she hadn't known, but like I said before, I didn't really blame her for not taking me seriously. It's like the boy who cried wolf, you know?

"After a couple of weeks there, the counselors decided it was best for me not to live with my mom, and definitely not with my dad. I went to a foster home, way out south of the city. And let me tell you, I hated it. It was a therapeutic foster home, which meant that they'd be helping deal with the problems the kids had. But the way they dealt with things was to read the Bible. It was really, really Christian, and for me it didn't have any hope of succeeding. There was no belief there on my part, so I resented those lectures, that Bible reading. In fact, the whole thing was kind of sickening to me."

Kara says that she got in with another bad group of friends

After Kara ran from her abusive father's house, she was placed in a religious foster home. Kara was turned off and eventually ran from the foster home, too.

when she lived at the foster home and that it wasn't long before she got into trouble.

"I had this friend, and the two of us just didn't care about school," she admits. "We'd get a bunch of kids together at lunch and just walk right out the door. I mean, there was no open lunch; we weren't supposed to leave. We just did. What were they going to do?

"Well, I guess they *did* do something, after a while," she says, laughing. "The police came looking for me when I had run once from the foster home. I'd taken a little backpack full of stuff and just had gone to my friend's house. I always had a backpack ready to go, just in case. And I knew my friend wouldn't care; her mom had no rules, either. In fact, it was a lot like my other friend, the one whose mom had a boyfriend she was always seeing.

"So anyway, the police came looking for me, and they found me. I got taken to another shelter, where I stayed a couple of weeks. I didn't mind that shelter; the kids were real nice. I didn't get along with this one counselor. She just went crazy on me when she caught me using the phone for a personal call. I just handled it by yelling back at her. I wasn't about to get yelled at like that by someone I didn't even know."

A FRIEND'S HOUSE

From the shelter, Kara was transferred back to the foster home. She left there for her friend's house within a few days.

"I knew I couldn't stand it there," she says. "I figured my friend was just hanging around, since both of us had gotten kicked out of the main high school. We'd been transferred to an alternative school, but that wasn't a whole lot better. We still skipped a lot, but at least we had each other to be with.

"And like always, I'd been in touch with my mom. And my social worker, too. I told my social worker where I was and how I didn't want to go back to that foster home. She told me I could stay at my friend's house until she could get me a placement in some other facility. She understood how unhappy I was.

"My mom . . . I didn't tell her where I was exactly. She knew I was safe, and that was all I told her. But what happened was really strange! I guess my social worker and my mom were in communication with each other, because not long afterwards I came home from the alternative school, and my mom was parked in the garage! I guess she'd gotten the address from my social worker, and she probably knew I'd have bolted if I'd seen her parked outside. So there she was, with my stuff all packed up, waiting in the garage.

"Where my placement was, I found out from my mom, was Lino Lakes Correctional Facility. It was like a prison for kids with big problems. So the two of us drove out there—quite a drive, let me tell you. Way north. It took a long time to get there, but it was kind of nice being with my mom again, at least for a little while."

Lino Lakes

The facility, says Kara, was very different from any notions she had had about what prisons for kids were like.

"The rooms were nice, carpeted, lots of wood. You have your own room, and your living area is shared by ten rooms. And the doors are locked from the inside, not the outside. They want to keep certain people out, I guess. They figure you're there to be helped, not necessarily punished. And besides, there's nothing but woods around the place, and I guess it wouldn't be a great idea to just go off without knowing what you were doing.

"When my mom first dropped me off, the staff took everything away from me—my clothes, money, jewelry, everything. I had to take a shower and put on this sweatsuit they gave me. It was red, and that tells everyone you are new. And people who've gotten in trouble at the prison, they get red, too. I guess red means you're sort of a risk for a while. That's when lots of people tend to bolt, right after they get there, the first twenty-four hours.

"The staff was really friendly. It's their job to help you work out all the stuff that's been making you get in trouble. So it wouldn't pay for them to be all mean and everything. All of the rooms in the mod—that's what they call each section, the mod—can be seen from the desk where the staff sits, right in the middle of the building. There's a mod for short-term girls, long-term girls (that's where I was), short-term boys, and long-term boys.

"Lots of the kids were there for serious stuff: robbery, assault, things like that. Lots for chemical dependency, and a huge number like me, for running. There's a school there. I made lots of friends there. Believe it or not, I'm pretty easy to get along with! I didn't know anyone when I arrived except this one boy who was the little brother of a friend of mine. That's all."

Were there rules that were easy to break at Lino Lakes? Kara shrugs and shakes her head uncertainly.

"It was really, really structured, so I don't think so. And to tell you the truth, I was trying to be good. Most of the staff were real gentle, but a couple of them could get in your face and yell. I laid low and didn't cause any trouble. I tried not to talk back to them, tried not to get into any skirmishes with anyone.

"If I'd been trying, I could have broken a few rules, maybe. Like we stayed with our own mod and didn't really socialize with other kids. Especially boys—that was forbidden. But you can pass notes. Like, if you're working in the laundry, you can put a note in the pocket of some boy's clothes if you want to get a message to him. I didn't do it. I didn't have anyone I wanted to talk to there, but I saw lots of other girls doing it.

"What I concentrated on was my treatment. See, everyone has stuff that they're dealing with there, stuff they want to work on. With me, I was learning about why I run. There's more to running than just running, I found out. There's anger, trust, lots of issues that aren't getting dealt with when I run. Nobody makes you work on stuff; they figure that by forcing someone, it would just be a waste of time. A person would just go through the motions, you know?

"But I was in a parent-teen group, discussing things about communication and trust and stuff like that. We'd never really talked about things like that before. My mom was in it, too. She'd make that long drive up twice a week for our individual sessions, and that was good. I was really proud of her, since that's such a long way to come. She was really committed to helping the two of us, I guess."

"I WANTED TO BE AN ADULT"

Kara finished her treatment and was released to her mother. She enrolled in an alternative school, which would give her more individual attention than a public school could.

"I had a new boyfriend, too," she says, smiling. "His name is Chad. He lived out south, where the alternative school was, and he went to the same school. He had lots of problems he was working on—his dad had taken off to California—so we saw a lot of each other. Too much, according to my mom.

"She didn't want me to get too involved with Chad. That's what she said, but I think differently. I thought she wasn't giving him a fair chance, mostly because she had liked my previous boyfriend. His name was Jason, and I'd met him through a friend when I was living at my dad's. He was nice, yeah. I mean, he used to write me these ten-page letters when I was in Lino. My mom thought he was really wonderful, really loyal.

"But I had broken up with Jason, for two reasons. First of all, I found out that he had been cheating on me, and I wasn't about to stand for that. And secondly, he had told me over and over that he was going to stop using drugs. But I heard from a friend that he had started back on them, so he lied. But as far as my mom was concerned, he was the best, and she was kind of mad that I'd broken up with him. Don't ask me why."

A close-up of Kara's monitor. While in Lino Lakes Correctional Facility, Kara worked to uncover the reasons why she ran away, and she and her mother began discussing those issues.

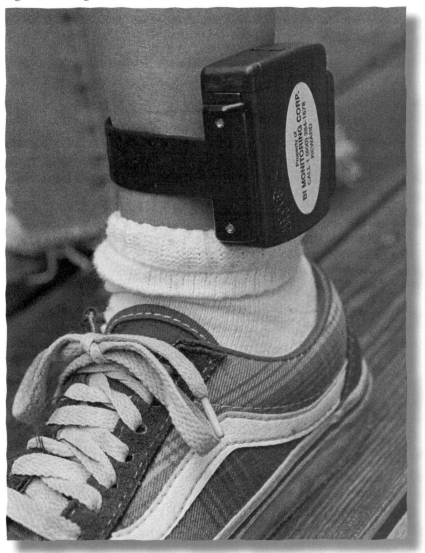

Kara enjoyed spending time with Chad and soon began staying out all night, clearly going against her mother's rules.

"I know it was against the rules," she explains. "But I wanted to be an adult. I was tired of her rules, tired of being told what to do all the time. I'd tell her, 'Okay, Mom, I'll be in by eleven,' and then I'd just do what I wanted—stay out all night, either with friends or just with Chad.

"That made her really mad, and we were fighting a lot. It was about six months after I'd been released that me and Chad ran away together, to my friend Mike's home."

LIVING WITH HER BOYFRIEND IN A TRAILER PARK

Mike lived with his parents in a trailer park about ten minutes away from the school Chad and Kara attended. It seemed like a safe place for them to stay, and Mike's parents were surprisingly agreeable to the arrangement.

"It sounds kind of funny, I guess," she admits. "His parents knew us, though. We'd been there to visit Mike after school other times. And they didn't look at the situation as if they were harboring fugitives. They just figured, 'We'd rather have those kids here than out on the streets getting in trouble or beat up or something.' I guess, too, that they didn't have much control. Mike pretty much got his own way all the time. Teenage boys are like that, I guess, pretty hard to control. Mike is hard to tell what to do.

"The trailer park was a good place for people who didn't want to run into police. See, it's private property, so the police aren't allowed down there to patrol. The sheriff can go, like, if there's a crime or a disturbance or something. But otherwise, nobody bothers you. So me and Chad were protected, and we stayed there for about a month.

"I called my mom as usual, to tell her I was safe and not to worry. She was upset, though. She thought that after Lino we'd be okay and we'd be able to work out these problems. So she'd do a lot of crying on the phone and beg me to tell her the number where I was. I didn't, though."

What did they do with their days? Kara looks thoughtful.

"We'd skip school, number one. And we'd drive into the city, hang around uptown, talk to people. It was kind of risky, now that I think about it, because there's a lot of weird stuff that goes on

Not long after her release from Lino Lakes, Kara met her boyfriend, Chad, and began staying out late with him. Fighting soon erupted between Kara and her mother, and Kara ran away again.

there, especially with drugs and stuff. But we were fine; we just stayed together.

"After about a month, though, money at the trailer was getting tight. It was expensive for Mike's parents to feed two extra people, and I felt sort of bad about that. Plus, it was really crowded, and I was getting pretty tired of sleeping on the floor all the time.

"So what I did was, I called my mom, asked her to pick me up.

Kara shows off her collection of paraphernalia from her favorite movie, Aladdin.

She came an hour or so later, to the top of the park. I met her there so she'd have no way of knowing which trailer I'd been staying in. I guess I figured in case I ever needed to come out here again, I didn't want her knowing, you see what I mean? I came home and unpacked most of my stuff. I did keep that back-pack ready, just in case."

A FIGHT LEADS TO DETENTION IN THE JUVENILE CENTER

Less than twenty-four hours later Kara's mother called the police and told them to take her daughter into custody.

"It was so stupid," Kara moans. "We got in this big argument, and it was so *childish*. I was sitting out on the deck, writing in my poetry journal. It's something I started during therapy, and it sort of helps me get things out of my system, you know? Anyway, I was smoking, too. And when we started arguing, she got so mad she picked up my pack of cigarettes and threw them over the balcony.

"I was mad, since it's such a long walk down to get them. Plus, you have to walk all the way around the back of the building. So before I went down, I grabbed her cigarettes and threw them, too. I went outside to retrieve mine, and I looked down the street, and here come two patrol cars! She'd called them on me!

"She'd told them I had hit her. That's the only way you can get a police officer to come. Otherwise, in arguments, they won't bother. So she'd lied, and here they came. I walked up to the cops, and I said, 'Are you here to get me?' They were trying to get me into the house to talk to my mom, but I didn't want to. I was sick of the whole thing and mad at my mom for what she had done."

Kara's mother met the police and her daughter at the front door. In her hands she had Kara's backpack.

"She told them she didn't want me coming back," remembers Kara. "She threw the backpack at me and told the cops to take me somewhere. I know now that we could have talked this out without even involving the police. But then—I was so angry, so betrayed. I blew my top, just went off on her. I was screaming and swearing at her and kicking and punching the cops. They handcuffed me and hog-tied me. That's where they tie something to my feet that connects behind my back to my handcuffs. I was carried to the police car and taken to the juvenile center downtown. I was charged, yeah, with disorderly conduct, obstructing legal process, and assault on an officer."

"NO PLACE FOR ME TO GO"

When she was processed at the juvenile center, Kara was taken to court, where the second and third charges against her were dropped. Still being charged with disorderly conduct, she awaited sentencing.

"I just stayed in juvenile; there was nowhere else to go," she says. "It was so boring there, nothing to do. My mom visited me there, but she kept insisting that she didn't think it would solve anything for me just to keep coming home. She said the same thing each time in court, too. She'd appear, just like she was supposed to, but three different court dates she refused to take me home. And still there was no place for me to go.

"I couldn't go to my mom's, couldn't go to my dad's. I was locked up in this little cell. They called it a room, but I know better—a cement desk and bed frame, a gross metal toilet right in your room. Everything was the same color, this dingy white cement. I'd watch out my window, look at the cars, and wish I was in them."

Finally, at her fourth appearance, Kara was told that she was being placed in a group home in the city. She stayed there only a week or so before she ran away.

"I found a friend, and the two of us were moving around a lot, just trying to stay away from the cops and away from trouble," she says. "I was in contact with my mom, like always. I told her I was on the north side, and that made her really nervous, because of all the drugs and crime up there."

"SOMETHING BAD HAPPENED"

"Eventually I split from my friend and went back south, to the trailer park. I didn't feel right going back to Mike's house. And Chad wasn't there anymore. He'd gotten in some trouble, I guess. So I went to this Korean family we'd gotten to know when Chad and I were there before.

"They had a trailer just up the hill from Mike's. I liked going there, mostly because they were Korean. Me and the girl and her brother would laugh about stuff that we found funny about living around white people. It was kind of nice to connect, you know?

"But something bad happened while I was there. I was raped—by the father. He was an alcoholic and wasn't there before when I got to know them. He and the mom were separated, but since he was the father of her children, she was letting him stay there for a little while.

"I was sleeping in the living room, and the girl and her mom were sharing a bed in the bedroom. I'm not sure where the father was supposed to be, but I woke up at, like, two in the morning, and he was on top of me. I couldn't scream: He told me that if I made a sound, he'd beat the blank-blank-blank out of me. I had a witness, though. There was a friend of the family sleeping in the next room (I told you it was crowded), and he heard what was going on. He was nineteen; I guess his parents had kicked him out. He didn't come to help me, but at least he verified my story later on."

Kara says she ran down the hill to Mike's trailer and woke his family up.

"I was really scared," she says. "I talked, and cried, and Mike and his mom were really great. His mom said, 'If we call the police, I want you to do the right thing: press charges.' I said that I would. That was no easy decision, either, because talking to the cops was risky for me. I was a fugitive. I had a warrant out for my

Kara decided to notify the police of her rape even though they had a warrant out for her arrest: "I didn't know exactly what was going to happen to me, but I knew I didn't want to let that guy get away with raping me."

arrest for running from a court-ordered placement. I didn't know exactly what was going to happen to me, but I knew I didn't want to let that guy get away with raping me."

SOMETHING CLICKED

The police took Kara's statement and, as she had predicted, took her into custody as well as the rapist. First she was taken to a hospital, where it was verified that she had indeed been raped.

"Then they took me to the sheriff's office to a holding cell and then transferred me back to juvenile," she says. "I was there awhile, until they could find a place for me to go, just like before. But this time, I was sent to a place that really seemed to help me. It was the County Home School, and maybe I was just in the right frame of mind or something, but it seemed to click for me there.

"It's a minimum-security corrections place, like a jail in some ways, but lots less secured than Lino had been. At Lino there was a big fence around the place, and we were more regimented. But here at the Home School, it was more free.

"You could wear regular clothes, so you didn't feel like an inmate so much. You stayed in cottages, twenty-four to a cottage. They were locked at night, but people moved around during the day. You went to school; there was a school right on the premises.

"The best thing, though," she says with a smile, "was the staff. I mean, they respected us, had fun with us, ate with us. It was like they were family. They called us by our first names, not our last names. I was in this sexual abuse group there, to work out some of the stuff that happened to me when I was raped. The victim advocate guy helped me press charges, and that was good.

"I felt like so much that had been bottled up inside me just came out. I felt like I grew up so much. It's hard to really explain, and I know I'm not doing a great job. It's just that all of a sudden, I was thinking, God, Kara, you're getting too old to keep running away all the time. Figure it out!"

RUNNING ONE LAST TIME

Her newfound maturity didn't kick in completely, she admits. Released after five months from the County Home School, she was sent to a group home and ran away yet again.

"I hated that place," she says bitterly. "It was like night and day from the Home School. The staff there never believed us, and I absolutely *hate* being wrongly accused of things. They thought that some of us were drinking and having sex with the boys there. But it didn't happen. And I'm telling the truth.

"So a couple of my friends and me, we left. And for a while we were just sort of moving around, place to place. I'd done that so much, and like I said before, I felt like I didn't want to live this way anymore. So I called my parole officer, and he said it would look a lot better if I turned myself in, so I did. I called my mom from downtown and said, 'Mom, I'm really ready to come home this time.'

"She came out and got me, and we just looked at each other. I told her I wanted to turn myself in, and she said, 'Let's go out and eat first.' So we did, just the two of us. We went to a pizza place I hadn't been to in so long. I can't tell you how good it tasted. I used to lose so much weight when I was running. I never had enough money, you know?"

Kara and her mother went to court soon afterward and were told that Kara had to go to a treatment school but that she could live with her mother during that time. In the meantime, she was told she would be placed on house arrest, which meant that she would be wearing the ankle monitor twenty-four hours a day.

After years of running away, Kara has found a new maturity and understanding and is now working on improving her relationship with her mother.

"Like I told you, it's a major inconvenience," she says. "A guy comes out every so often, just pops in. He wants to make sure that I'm being good, not having any visitors. And they have a computer downtown that calls the monitor here automatically and tells them I'm here all the time.

"One night about a week ago I was upstairs watching TV, and my mom was downstairs. And the next morning they called from the police station, telling us they had twelve minutes of unmonitored time. They asked if I'd taken off the monitor! My mom was really surprised, and she said, 'I'm glad I was home. I might not have believed you about this one!' Trust issues with us, you know.

"Anyway, I'm going to be getting this off in a couple of days, and that will be great. I've got some things I want to do—not big things, but just some stuff. Like my little cousin just got her license, and we're going to do something right after I get this off. She's class of '98, and I'm '97. But I'm not graduating this year with my class. No way. I've missed too much school this year. And it's so weird that she's got her license before me! I'm really jealous."

"I'M READY TO WORK THINGS OUT"

Kara is very glad about one thing—that the man who raped her was sent to prison.

"I was worried at first," she admits. "He kept pleading not guilty. But right before he went to trial, he ended up pleading guilty. So I didn't have to appear in court; it was all settled. He got nine years in prison. If he is good there, he'll be out in six years. But the way I figure, I'll be twenty-three by then, and probably he won't be able to find me, if that's what he's planning to do."

Kara is confident about something else—that she has come to the end of her running-away days.

"I know it's hard to believe." She smiles. "But so many people have told me, 'Grow up.' And I think it's partly an age thing and partly I'm ready to work things out. Things they told me at Lino and at the Home School . . . things are really sinking in.

"My mom and I won't ever be the best of friends, but we'll get along. I really love her, and I know I've been a handful. We get along okay now. We have little arguments, but nothing turns into a major battle like before. I feel like we don't have an adult-kid relationship now; it's more adult-adult. I don't feel angry inside. I've really turned a corner. I know that, and I'm going to prove it."

As for long-term plans, Kara has a few.

"I'll live here until I'm eighteen," she says. "And then I'd like to go to college. Know what I'm planning to be? A JCW—a juvenile corrections worker!" She laughs. "I've seen so many bad ones that I really know from experience how to do it right. Plus, I've seen at Home School how to be really effective with kids. I didn't respect authority before I went there. I guess I didn't plan on getting turned around, trusting people that much. I'm just glad it happened."

Marvin

"THERE'S A BIG STEEL DOOR THAT
CLICKS, AND THEN YOU'RE
LOCKED UP, MAN. . . . AND THE
ONLY THING TO DO IS SIT ON
YOUR BED AND LOOK OUT THE
WINDOW AT THE CLOCK. . . . ALL
THE ROOMS IN JUVENILE CENTER
FACE THAT CLOCK. EVERYONE I
KNOW WATCHED IT. AND MAN, IT
MOVED SO SLOW! ALL NIGHT,
SOMETIMES I'D WATCH."

Marvin is a good-looking boy and far older and more self-possessed than most sixteen-year-olds. He is black, yet he is living with a white family in one of the most homogeneous white suburbs of the city—a situation that might make many black teenagers uncomfortable—and he likes it just fine.

"Yeah, I guess it was sort of a culture shock at first," he says, smiling. "I'm getting used to it, though. I've lived here at Nancy's house for about a month. Nancy's the one who ran the Second Chance Ranch, the group home where I was staying. When it was time for me to leave there, I wrote a letter to the judge, asking if it would be all right if after I got out of there, I could come here. Nancy had already told me it would be fine with her, that she would like having me stay here."

It is certainly not a usual thing for a juvenile offender to live in the home of his warden after his release from the institution. It is not the average set of circumstances. But Marvin is certainly not an average sort of boy.

"I trust her," he says simply. "I guess because I was at the ranch for so long. She cared about the kids there, and that was a new thing for me, to have somebody caring about me. I just felt like if I could stay with her, I'd have a better chance of being able to stay out of trouble. So being here with Nancy and her family . . . it's going to be a really good thing for me."

How did a troubled kid with a record of drug dealing, assault, and gang activity end up turning his life around? Marvin says he credits many of the people he came into contact with in the justice system.

MAKING LOTS OF MONEY

He started out on Chicago's south side, living with his parents and his eight brothers and sisters. If you had to find a point where trouble really started, he says, it was back in Chicago, when he was eleven or twelve.

"That was when I started selling drugs," he says. "My mom was doing drugs herself. I don't think she had a clue that I was selling, making money that way. But boy, I did. The kind of money I made back then was unbelievable for a fifth-grade kid.

"It wasn't hard, no. Not at all. You just start. I was selling rocks—you know, crack. And cocaine, too. I started out because of one of my older brother's friends. He gave me some to sell. It was in an apartment building, too, so I didn't have to go nowhere. I didn't even leave my apartment, that's how easy it was. People just came to me, knocked on the door, and there I was. I don't really know how everybody knew to come to me. I guess it was just word of mouth. But they did come, that's for sure.

"I made between two and three hundred dollars a day. I was getting some help from my friends, too. They'd come in the apartment and help me, sit around with me. It was a lot of money, more than a little kid has a right to be making. No real work to it, and no real risk, either. I mean, I didn't have to worry about hiding it or going around the blocks and maybe being stopped by a policeman or something."

What does an eleven-year-old do with so much money? Marvin looks perplexed.

"I don't know! I mean, I was thinking about that the other day, how I've got no money. I mean, I got a part-time job and everything, but it pays nothing like I used to earn in a morning back on

Marvin got his start selling crack and cocaine at eleven years old, when his older brother's friend gave him some to sell. He says, "The kind of money I made back then was unbelievable for a fifth-grade kid."

the south side. In a way, I wish I'd put some of it aside. I must have wasted most of it. I bought stuff—food, clothes. Just used it up.

"Drugs? No, not me. I've seen too many people doing that stuff, and I knew enough to be scared of it. The way my mom and dad acted when they were doing crack, the last thing I'd have been doing was smoking that money up, doing drugs."

NOT REALLY A MOM

Marvin says it was his parents' drug use, especially his mother's, that really contributed the most to his problems growing up.

"My mom wasn't really a mom," he says. "She would leave for three or four days at a time. And I had a lot of kids to be responsible for. I mean, I didn't really worry about my two older brothers. They were teenagers; they could take care of themselves, supposedly. But I had six younger brothers and sisters, so I had to be taking care of them since my mom wasn't doing nothing about us.

"I wasn't much of a cook, and there wasn't usually anything in the house to eat, so I'd walk over to my grandmother's house a lot. She lived about a mile and a half away. She'd give me some food or maybe a little money to take back home to feed my brothers and sisters and me. So we ate, anyway. And sometimes it was nice weather, and I'd take the kids over to my grandma's with me. We'd all go.

"But things kept getting worse and worse at home," he says. "I thought a lot about going to my mom or my dad and saying something. I'd practice what I was going to say when I was alone. I wanted to tell them how bad they were being as parents and how we kids didn't have a chance. It was so hard, and there was nobody acting like no adult in the whole house. But I never did it. I got mad when I was by myself, and I felt real brave. But I was scared to talk to them, especially to my dad. I guess I didn't think it was my business, so I just stayed out of the way most of the time."

Marvin says the drug use was so frequent that it seemed to him there was never a time when both his parents were coherent.

"It's easy to tell," he says. "I mean, not so much in how they'd act, but in how they didn't act. You know, they didn't act like you were there at all. Or you could smell the smoke. Or once in a while, especially at first, my mom would act strange if I came into her room, and she'd quick start cleaning up, like she wanted to hide what she was doing. You could just tell."

A DEADLY SHOOTING

His family ended up leaving Chicago, he says, because of the murder of one of his uncles. "See, he was this big-time drug dealer. And when I was about twelve, he and my mom were going somewhere one day, and one of his friends was driving them around. He pulled over and lifted the hood up. I guess the deal was that it was some kind of signal, that the guy that was driving them was working for someone else.

"Anyway, some men came up real fast and shot my uncle six times in the head, like an assassination. And they shot my mom twice, right in the head. My mom didn't die, though, and that was something these guys hadn't thought about. She survived because of the way her hair was done up in ponytails. The bullets deflected off the bands she was using. They didn't go deep enough to get into her brain, or whatever. I mean, she was hurt, but they saved her life. They couldn't do nothing for my uncle, though. He died on the way to the hospital."

Because the police were concerned that Marvin's mother was still in some danger, they urged her to get away from the city for a while. So after she was released from the hospital, she and her family moved north.

"See, they didn't catch the dudes that done it right away," says Marvin, "and the police figured that those guys knew where we lived and everything. It was risky, so they told us to leave. We all came up here to live, even my one older brother. The other older brother, the oldest one, he was in prison for armed robbery. He'd used a gun and tried to steal some lady's car.

"Anyway, they ended up catching the dudes that shot my mom and my uncle, and my mom was going back and forth to Chicago for the trial. They ended up putting them in prison because she was the eyewitness."

DIFFICULT CHANGE

Marvin was just starting seventh grade when he and his family moved from Chicago. He remembers that things were difficult in his new home.

"At first we didn't have no real place to live," he says. "So we stayed downtown in a shelter for about two months. Then we moved over to the north side of the city when we finally got a place to live. But things went wrong. The place we had found had lead paint in there, and my little brothers and sisters were chewing on it, I think. And so we moved back to the shelter for a while and found another place. And the same thing happened with the lead paint.

"They were just bad places," he says with a sigh. "They were real old, real dirty. Nobody had bothered to fix them up, even a little bit. But people figure, 'Hey, some poor family will come in here if they got no choice.' And that's what happened. But at least we didn't stay too long at those places.

"One of the hardest things then was trying to go to school. We were always in a different place, so we never knew if a bus would pick us up or not. They was supposed to be sending the buses, but sometimes they didn't know we'd moved, and the bus wouldn't come. Or it would come to the old house, and we'd moved out of it already. Lots of times it wouldn't show up at the shelter, and there were lots of kids there who were waiting, same as me.

"When I did go, school wasn't too fun. I ended up getting in

Marvin's family left Chicago when his uncle, a major drug dealer, was murdered. The police thought Marvin's mother, who had also been shot but survived, was in danger, and the family moved.

more trouble, I guess. It wasn't because of the schoolwork, though I didn't do much of that. I think I was smart enough, but no one at my house really cared about whether you did your homework, or were on time for school, or even whether you showed up at all. I didn't care, either."

Marvin says that he was frequently in trouble at school for starting fights, a charge he fully admits. "I got kicked out of several schools for fighting," he says. "Fault? I don't know, probably mostly my fault. I never thought about it in terms of who was to blame. Most fights were just stupid; someone would say something to me, and I'd start punching. Or a food fight in the cafeteria at lunch. Somebody throws some food at a table I'm sitting at, and pretty soon we throw stuff back, and a bunch of us get caught."

He smiles. "I got caught a lot, I guess."

During this time, Marvin got involved with a gang called the Gangster Disciples, or the Folk, as they were sometimes called.

"I'd been a GD back in Chicago, when I was eleven," he says.

"It wasn't really a big deal back then; it was more just a bunch of kids to hang around with. We didn't really get in too much trouble in Chicago. It was just for the company, you know?

"But here, it was different. I mean, it wasn't too hard getting in with the GDs here. They were at the shelter downtown, they were at the schools I went to. It's not hard to spot them, no. I mean, someone's got their hat cocked to the right, and you got your hat cocked to the right, and you're, like, 'What's up?' and they're, like, 'What's up?' And I was wearing blue and black. It's not hard to see, when it's the Folks.

"I didn't think of myself as being real fierce, at least at first. Sure, I carried a pistol, but I'd had guns since I was eleven. I didn't carry a gun to school or anything like that. It was too risky. But guns were easy to get, and everybody expected you to have one, especially when you were hanging around."

"EVERYTHING WAS HARD"

His mother and father were still heavy drug users, and Marvin was spending more and more time on the streets with his friends in the gang.

"Everything was hard then," he remembers. "My parents were probably worse off because of the stress from the trial and everything. I don't know . . . maybe that's an excuse. But everything was bad, and nothing was changing. Nobody was doing nothing about it, you know? School was bad, home was bad. Nobody told me to straighten around. I wouldn't have listened, anyway. I'm sure of that.

"Things kind of got worse when some friends of mine, some GDs, formed this little set, kind of an offshoot of the gang, I guess you could say. We started out just me and my brother and some of my friends, you know, kind of thinking that maybe it would be cool to do some music, be a rap group. We'd be sitting around, you know, and we'd be rapping, just making stuff up as we went along. We'd do a little rhythm to it. It sounded pretty good to us.

"So we thought that would be cool, just make some money doing that. We came up with a name for ourselves, too: the SKM— Street Knowledge Mafia. That was our rap group name. But after about three weeks, we realized that wasn't going to happen. Nobody was going to take us serious, so it just faded away.

"Anyway, what I meant about getting worse, was that we

The move from Chicago was difficult for Marvin; the family had no permanent home, and he would often miss school. He got in trouble frequently for fighting, and eventually joined a gang.

started changing the idea of the SKM to more of a money-making organization. I guess you could call it a gang. It doesn't really matter. It kind of started operating like that, I guess.

"There were people like me, Folks. And my brother; he was a Vice Lord. And some other Vice Lords that we knew. We all got along, so the gang affiliations didn't matter. It didn't matter what [affiliation] we claimed, anyway. I mean, look at me and my brother. We're in different gangs, but we don't care. Hey, he's my blood. I'm there for him long before I'd be there for any GD. That's just how it goes, you know.

"Anyway, the SKM started growing. We had lots of guys asking us what we were about, like they wanted to join us. We'd just hang with a guy for a while, chill a little. We'd see if we liked him, if it seemed like he was down with the same stuff we was. If it seemed cool, we'd ask him to join us. I mean, we didn't want no mass murderer, you know, getting us all a bad reputation, getting us all in trouble."

Marvin says that the SKM didn't bother with a lot of the trappings that other gangs used.

His home and school life in shambles, Marvin formed a new group with some friends—an organization like a gang, but one that focused on making money.

"We didn't mess with colors, no graffiti, no painting around," he says. "We thought that would be kind of stupid. We did have signs, but real easy—just SKM, like this." He makes finger gestures in the approximate shapes of the three letters. "We'd throw up stuff like that, that's all.

"And so there ended up being like nineteen or twenty of us. And more and more people kept being interested. They'd ask us if they could be down with whatever we were doing. Making money, that was the main thing. That was what we'd tell them."

DEALING DRUGS

For Marvin and his fellow SKMs, "making money" translated into selling drugs. He was as successful at it as he had been back in Chicago as a child.

"We'd hooked into a couple of people right off who could supply us with the drugs we needed," he explains. "We just had to do the rest. It wasn't hard to get people to help us out. Like I said before, it's one of the easiest ways to make money in the whole world. There are lots of buyers out there, don't forget. Lots of people in this world that do drugs—lots of businessmen, kids on their way to school, mothers. Lots of people.

"The way I did it was to just explore, just get myself noticed, let people see me. That way you get known fast. You have the stuff in your sock, or maybe your pocket. Like for reefer [marijuana] I'd be up at the corner, maybe sitting on one of those bus stop benches. I'd just do like this." He puts his thumbnail and forefinger together near his mouth, as though he is smoking.

"And somebody comes up to you in a minute or so. They ask you what you're about, what you got. So you tell them, and you give them your pager number, whatever. Then that guy comes back the next day, and maybe his friends, too. I get on my bike, get noticed in other places. Pretty soon word really gets around.

"And, like, one of our friends had a spot—a house or apartment—and we used that to sell out of. I was making good money and not working very hard. Maybe five hundred dollars in a few hours. If I'd wanted to earn more, I could have done more. I didn't feel like sitting around, though. That's all I cared to do, just because I was scared of police and stuff. So a few hours was fine for me."

"I'M NOT TAKING IT NO MORE"

It was during this time that Marvin's mother was arrested and sent to the county workhouse for a year. Marvin's father decided to move his family back to Chicago for a while.

"She'd been stealing stuff, and she got caught. I guess she'd steal the stuff and bring it back to get cash. It was for her drugs," Marvin explains. "So we went back to Chicago to live, and that was real bad. I was mad all the time, it seemed like. Nobody was ever home. My dad was out selling drugs and stuff, and I'd be the only one there with the little kids. The house was always trashed; we never had no food. I was glad when the year was up, and my mom got out.

"When my mom got released and we moved back, things were okay for a little while. She seemed a little better, and maybe she was paying more attention to us. But, I don't know, things went downhill after that. It didn't last too long, that good time."

Marvin says that as his relationship with his mother deteriorated even more, he became more and more angry, and he was starting to turn that anger on her.

"She'd been abusing us for so long—emotionally, physically—I was getting real tired of it," he says. "I mean, she was either in, like, a coma, not even caring about anything, or being real mean. She'd hit us, yell at us, and call us names. Just like my father did, and he did that a lot.

"So what I did, is tell her, 'Look, I'm not going to respect you any more unless you start respecting me. And that's a fact. I'm not taking it no more, and I'm not watching the little kids take it, either.' But she didn't listen, she didn't change. So then I started doing back to her what she was doing to me. I'd start hitting right back or yelling right back when she did it. She'd hit me with an extension cord; I'd grab it right back. That's the way things got at our house."

"A No-Win Situation"

As Marvin became more assertive, his mother's anger only increased. And as that happened, he felt more and more that he was alone. "I never felt like she loved me, not ever," he says quietly. "She either was whupping us, or she was acting like she didn't care. And if I would stick up for my little brothers and sisters, I would get hit more than ever. It was a no-win situation. I could have run away, I guess, but I didn't know where. Maybe my grandma's on my dad's side, but not for long. And my grandma on my mom's side . . . forget it. She'd probably be doing the same drugs as my mom. She's the same way, the same way.

"I thought about talking to someone. I almost talked to my dad, but what was the use of that? He didn't act like he cared, either. And there was nobody at school for me to talk with. I mean, there probably was, but I have never been the type of person to share my feelings with anyone. So I just kept that anger bottled up. Even when I was getting mad at my mom, I was only letting a little of my anger out.

"The result of all this stuff is that she started calling the cops on me. I'd get mad and push her back or grab something out of her hand so she didn't hit me with it, and she'd call them. And I'd get taken downtown for a while to the juvenile center. I guess I was there a week or two, never more than that. And then she'd agree to let me come home. I was there maybe seven times, at most."

The final episode came when Marvin and his cousin got into a fight, and his mother called the police. Then, says Marvin, he was taken away from home—for good.

Marvin's relationship with his mother worsened when he began standing up to her. "She'd been abusing us for so long—emotionally, physically—I was getting real tired of it," Marvin says.

A Boring Stay at the Juvenile Center

"It was stupid how it happened," he says. "I was playing Nintendo with my little cousin. I was going to throw the controller to him, but it hit my older cousin—the eighteen-year-old—in the forehead. I mean, not even hard! So he hit me, and I hit him back, and like that. My mom called the cops, and I was taken out. And the thing is, I was sort of happy, because I got out of there, away from home.

"I wasn't happy about where I was going, though. It was the juvenile corrections center. Like I said before, I'd been there several times in the past. But this time, it was going to be for a long time—way more than two weeks.

"The place is really boring," he says, shaking his head. "I think it's supposed to be, so you have time to think about what you did. There's a big steel door that clicks, and then you're locked up, man. The rooms are tiny. But what do you need space for? There's nothing to do. There's steel toilets, and the rooms are really cold. A hard mattress, concrete bedstand. A little plastic mirror, a small toothbrush they give you, and small toothpaste. A concrete desk to sit at, to write if you want to.

"You wear a hospital suit, and blue is the only color they let you have. And the only thing to do is sit on your bed and look out the window at the clock. It's the only thing that has a color; the hands are lit up in neon lights. The clock is on the government center, I think. All the rooms in juvenile center face that clock. Everyone I know watched it. And man, it moved so slow! All night, sometimes I'd watch."

Waiting for a Court Date

Marvin says that his primary activity at the center was to wait for his court date. That, too, came slowly. "I went four or five times," he says. "And they denied me the right to go home. I was a menace to society, they said, because I could cause bodily harm to others and probably would. I was a risk. My mom and dad never even came, not even when they were supposed to for the court date. That was hard for me to understand.

"So I kept waiting. The days were long and the routine was boring. Eat breakfast, clean up your room. You have to take naps, just like a baby. If you do something wrong, you get locked in your room for a whole day. Like one time I got into a fight with some guy, and I got punished by being locked in my room for seven days. No breaks.

"Sometimes there was TV from 8:00 until bedtime at 10:00. Sometimes a movie on the VCR. But you couldn't leave. There were no privileges at all."

As Marvin's stay stretched to four months, his social worker became irritated. "He said that juvenile center wasn't supposed to be no long-term place," says Marvin. "He wanted me to get placed somewhere, so I could start living. Sitting around waiting for something that wasn't going to happen was stupid. So he got me transferred out of there to a children's home.

"That's when I met Nancy. No, she didn't work there; she ran this group home outside of town. She was there because she was supposed to interview some kid about coming to the group home, but he wasn't there at the children's home. I guess it was some mix-up. Anyway, she asked me, instead, if I would like to come there to live. It was called the Second Chance Ranch, she said."

THE RANCH

Marvin agreed to try the Second Chance Ranch, but it was only because he was so bored at the juvenile center.

"It was either that or stay at the center, and who knew how long that would be?" Marvin says. "I didn't ask; I didn't care. Nancy had told me that it was a good alternative, and it might work for me. But to be real honest, I didn't want to be there. It was just one more prison, one more jail, to me. So while she was busy talking to

Arguing with his mother led to several brief stays in juvenile prison. Marvin's final stay lasted for months as he awaited his court date, at which his parents did not appear.

me about it, telling me all the things about being there, I wasn't really listening. I didn't want to go nowhere but out, you know?

"I mean, you aren't with your friends, you aren't at home, somebody you don't know is telling you what to do. This ranch was just a prison that didn't have as many locks. All I knew was that I had to do what they said, and to me, that ain't being free.

Marvin was transferred to a children's home, where he met Nancy, who invited him to live at the group home she ran. He arrived at the Second Chance Ranch bitter and rebellious, but the staff patiently counseled him, chipping away at his tough exterior.

But my parole officer agreed to it, said it would be a good option for me. And after court, since I wasn't going to be allowed to go home anymore, I said okay.

"It was a long ride out there, real far from the city, I thought. There were about fourteen kids there, all boys. There were enough counselors there so that everyone would get a lot of one-on-one attention, and that was real good, I found out. They had horses there. I guess it was a real ranch."

Marvin says that while the ranch wasn't as structured and confining as the juvenile center had been, there were still strict routines.

"I mean, they don't let you just do what you want, run around and have fun. If that's what people think, they're really wrong," he says with a smile. "There's activities you can choose to do, that's true. But everybody was expected to do his share of the work to keep the place running. There was always some job that had to be done, and Nancy and the counselors weren't shy about assigning them to us. I don't ever remember working so hard as I did there."

"THE CHALLENGE WAS INSIDE ME"

During the week the routine was fairly simple. The boys were required to attend school, not at the ranch, but at the high school in town. "At first I didn't go, because I had home tutoring," he explains. "They had to get me up to speed so I could handle myself doing work at the level I was supposed to be at. And after school there were chores to do, cleaning, or whatever.

"I admit I was a little bit of a problem for the first four months I was there. I had myself an attitude; I was busy rebelling against them. I cussed at them, refused to cooperate. I didn't run away or get into fights because I figured if I did that, there'd be no hope the next time. I'd just get sent to a worse place. So I stayed put and decided to fight it through on my own. But it took me a while to get into it, yeah.

"See, the challenge was inside me. There were no locks on the doors, so if I'd wanted to run, it wouldn't have been too hard. And that's the thing, because you got to figure out that running isn't going to solve anything. It's a place where you are, and if you want to stay there, you got to follow their rules. It's simple to understand, but it's hard to accept, you know? And so, like I said, at first I didn't accept it. But then, these counselors and everybody are in your face so long, talking to you, being patient with you, refusing to let you go off and be alone, that I kind of wore down. I finally realized I better start talking to them."

Everyone at the ranch has issues that they decide to work on while they are there. For Marvin, it was his anger. "Everybody has a treatment program that fits what they need," he says. "They got to be working on something at the ranch. Otherwise they aren't going to get any better. I was going to work on my anger, my temper, and how it related to my family problems. They got a therapist up there, and your family can come out and she'll help you work out things together."

Marvin looks down. "My mom only got to come out twice, though. Twice in eleven months. She just didn't have no way of getting out there; they had to come out and pick her up. My dad never even came once.

"But I really helped myself in that program. First of all, the counselors would talk to me when I got mad. They encouraged me to express what I was thinking. I mean, I *never* talked things out before, not anything like that! One thing I learned, too, is that there are lots of healthy ways to express yourself. I mean, not just talking. That was limiting for me, I guess.

"My best way, I found out, was by writing. I've saved letters, copies of letters I wrote to my mom when I was at the ranch, letters I wrote to the judge, letters sometimes that I never even mailed. It just helped me, though, just writing it down and getting the words out."

EXPRESSING SCRAMBLED FEELINGS

Marvin offers a small stack of things he's written: lists of things he'd like to change, poems, and letters he's never sent.

"Dear Mom," one letter begins, "I want to be good to myself, but it's easier said than done. Sometimes it's hard to stop reliving the rotten times in my life. And it's not always easy to stop resenting and blaming others for everything that has happened to me."

He goes on to list for his mother some of the things that were most painful for him growing up.

"Mom, when we were little, you were never there. Mom, when friends are over, you talk about me or embarrass me so much. Or when I'm on the phone and you get on the other extension and say, 'Let me use the f—— phone,' or 'Get off the damn phone.' Mom, when I used to play basketball, you never came to one of my games. Everybody's moms and dads were there except mine. Mom, I think the thing that hurt me the most was the drugs. Because we never had nothing, somedays we used to worry about what we was going to eat. That hurt me."

Also in the letters, Marvin is quick to take the blame for his own anger and the problems it caused.

"I get a burning feeling inside of me whenever I have a problem with my family. . . . It's scary. I can't look anybody in the eye, because I'm afraid they'd see it. I felt like smashing the world into little pieces, [because] my mom was on drugs, and she didn't care what happens to me. I wanted to yell at the top of my lungs, but I just boiled inside instead. Or sometimes I used to run away into my own little dream world. It kept me from hurting so much. I'd dream about being a movie star, or a hero, or just about being special in someone else's life."

Marvin realized that anger was the main issue he needed to confront. Writing down his feelings gave him a healthy outlet for his anger and an effective way to manage it.

"When I was worked up about my problems," he concludes in one letter, "anything would set me off. If someone looked at me the wrong way, or said something I didn't want to hear, I'd blow up. . . . I took out my frustrations by beating them up."

"I FELT LIKE I WAS SOMEBODY"

As he learned to control his anger, Marvin began finding success where it had long eluded him, both in school and in the relationships he was forming with other people.

"I was really getting established," he says. "I was getting all A's in school, doing well. I mean—me—getting a 4.0! It was something I never thought I could do or even wanted to do. But now I was doing it, and I was enjoying how it felt.

"I really started liking myself. I mean, I didn't have good feelings before; my mom always put us kids down, told us how worthless we were. I used to be kind of chubby, and she'd always call me a fat pig and call my other brothers and sisters names, too. And my friends . . . she'd call them things. But when I'd been at the ranch awhile, I don't know, I felt like I was *somebody*. I do good at school, and people notice. It's hard to explain.

"A lot of it maybe is getting older and not so immature. And having friends who really like you, who do the same kind of things you're doing: studying, playing on teams, stuff like that. It was like they were sort of positive influences in my life, and they made me feel positive about myself."

Marvin admits that at first he had had reservations about going to that particular school. As one of the few students of color, he worried that he would be singled out for harsh treatment.

"It's white here, that's a fact," he shrugs. "It's funny, too, because before I came here, I remember one of my friends talking about this ranch and the high school here, the one I'm going to now. And he was telling everybody how racist it is, how everybody is down on black kids there. I mean, in the whole school, there are maybe six black kids. But I don't know . . . I was ready for the worst, but I never had any trouble like that. People seemed like they treated me fair.

"I won't tell you it wasn't hard," he cautions. "I mean, coming from an all-black school, or at least mostly black, there were some things to get used to. And I could have gotten in the situation where I could have gone back to the city and done that again. But

Marvin's resolved anger allowed him to enjoy life: "I really started liking myself. I mean, I didn't have good feelings before; my mom always put us kids down, told us how worthless we were."

I didn't want to. And it's not that I needed a *white* school; I just needed a place that was different, where nobody's expecting me to be a certain way. That's what."

"DANG! HOW DO THEY ALL KNOW ME?"

Besides his outstanding work as a student, Marvin has been gaining recognition as a gifted athlete.

"I play football and basketball, and I love it." He grins. "I'm on the varsity teams, doing real good. I even got a scrapbook here, where I keep all the clippings and stuff from the paper that mentions me."

He walks quickly to a shelf in the dining room and brings back a large album, already stuffed with articles and pictures: Marvin dunking the basketball, Marvin leading the team in rebounds, Marvin setting school records on the football field.

"It's funny, because I never did this good before," he says. "There aren't any other distractions in my life, so that helps. And for once, my grades are good enough so I'm eligible. I've already heard from coaches at universities and colleges. I'm only a sophomore; I got two more years to go!

"I know that I'm going to college. I'd go even if I didn't have the possibility of scholarships for sports. The thing is, you want to have options. The more options you got, the more in control of your life you can be. I mean, it's just like having all these friends now. As soon as I came here, it was basketball season, so that was lucky. I got on the team, and pretty soon, the whole school knew me.

"I was, like, Dang! How do they all know me? Everywhere it was 'Hey, Marvin!' I didn't think it would happen that fast. And the parents . . . they're cool, too. I know that a lot of it is that I'm good in sports. Maybe if I was just some guy, not helping the team win or anything, maybe they wouldn't care at all about me. But the thing is, that's who I am. I am good in sports.

"And I am helping the team," he says happily. "Listen, I took my team to the state tournament last year in basketball. I'm a guard—average about eighteen or nineteen points a game. My number? 45."

He leans over and points out a picture in the scrapbook. "Yeah, that's a good picture, but the one on the next page is better. Hopefully there'll be lots more next year. It's something I really look forward to, playing those games. Even practice is fun, but I wouldn't admit that to the coach."

"I Know I'm Loved"

At the end of his eleven months at the ranch, Marvin was told he could return to his home. It was a possibility that once would have made him happy, but this time he turned it down.

"I was thinking, yeah, maybe I could do that," he remembers. "But the truth is, I didn't want to. By this time I'm established at the school, have my friends, I've got sports, good grades. And people are asking me, 'Hey, Marvin, what are you going to be when you grow up?' I'll tell you, nobody ever asked me that before. I'd just look at them and say, 'I don't know, I don't know.'

"So, like I explained at first, I wrote that letter [to the judge]. I told him how much I'd learned and how nice Nancy had been to me. And the judge said okay. So I came here, and it's been real nice,

Marvin plays both varsity basketball and football, and his talent has earned him public recognition, as well as the attention of college coaches. Marvin says college is definitely in his future.

real nice. Nancy's got this nice house, and her family is great. She's going to be getting remarried soon, and I'm invited to the wedding. She's got kids and everything from another marriage, and we get along fine. I've got a home here for the next two years, until I graduate. Nancy treats me like a son, and I like that. I feel like I'm responsible, and she trusts me. I know I'm loved, like I belong."

What about his family back in the city?

"Things have changed," he says. "My mom is straight; she's been straight for a year. I respect her in a way, and I hold no grudges. See, the drugs were most of her personality, so it's hard to be mad at someone who wasn't even herself. I go home about every weekend to see them, and that's fine. She's proud of me, yeah. I mean, I'm going to be the first one out of our family ever to graduate from high school.

Marvin now maintains two homes: He lives with Nancy, where he is known as a gifted athlete and accomplished student, and he spends weekends with his mother, who is off drugs.

"It's like two worlds, going back and forth. I like seeing my brothers and sisters and seeing my mom. I got a girlfriend back there, too. I'll probably invite her up for dances next year. This year, yeah, I got invited to dances. A lot of girls here asked, but I didn't go. Didn't want to hurt anyone's feelings, I guess.

"Sometimes when I'm here, I really miss being there. I mean, I can live here forever and still not be used to certain things. I know that. Foods, the way people talk, everything. But it's not bad; it's just that I feel like I'm a little bit away from where I've always been. But to be honest, sometimes when I'm home, I get lonesome for being here. It goes both ways."

"IT WAS ME"

Marvin says that if he had to pinpoint one thing that turned him around from his trouble-bound life, he wouldn't even stop to think.

"It was me," he says simply. "That changed. More than anybody, more than anything. When they taught me about controlling my anger, when Nancy talked to me about writing and listening to myself inside, that changed me, and so I changed. I heard what they were saying, and I did it. I think sometimes people hear the right answers, but they're not ready to really listen. But I was ready, finally.

"I wrote those letters, those poems. And then, sitting around, reading all that stuff, thinking about all the stuff that happened to me . . . I don't know. It just hit me, really hit me. I started thinking: I want to be somebody else. I want to grow up and be somebody else."

Epilogue

There have been changes in the lives of the young people whose stories are included in *The Other America: Teens in Prison* between their first interviews and publication.

Kara says that the changes in her life are pretty minimal. She got bored with her job as a housekeeper at a nearby motel, and quit. She is in school, and is hoping to finish by next spring. She and her mother are getting along better, and Kara has quit running away.

Marvin is doing very well. He is the star athlete at his high school, having scored three touchdowns in the football season opener. He has been featured in the local newspaper as the leading yard gainer for his team. His grades are good, and he is socializing more on weekends with his teammates and school friends. What pleases him most, he says, is that his mother has been able to attend more than half of his games this fall.

Martin and his family no longer live in their house by the freeway. Residents of the house say they have no idea where the family lives, only that they left in a hurry.

Maniac, too, is unreachable. His phone and pager have both been disconnected, and a friend of his claims that he has not seen him in more than a month.

Ways You Can Get Involved

THE FOLLOWING ORGANIZATIONS CAN BE CONTACTED FOR MORE INFORMATION ABOUT TEENS IN PRISON AND THE JUVENILE JUSTICE SYSTEM.

Alternatives to Gang Membership (AGM)
City of Paramount
16400 Colorado Ave.
Paramount, CA 91723

This organization works toward the goal of eliminating the source of future gang membership by teaching young people the harmful consequences of the lifestyle. AGM has developed a school curriculum including the topics of self-esteem, nonviolent resolution of disputes, and the impact of children's gang affiliation on families.

National Association of Counsel for Children (NACC)
1205 Oneida St.
Denver, CO 80220

The NACC was founded in 1977 to enhance the well-being of children by promoting excellence in the field of children's law. Of special importance to this organization is working towards the improvement of the legal protection and representation of children.

National Council on Crime and Delinquency
685 Market St., Suite 620
San Francisco, CA 94105

This independent, nonprofit group attempts to educate the public on the need for prison reform, and to develop alternative methods of punishment for offenders.

The Sentencing Project
918 F St. NW, Suite 501
Washington, DC 20004

This organization offers various books and pamphlets stressing the need for different methods of sentencing for offenders, as well as information on prisoners' rights.

For Further Reading

Falcon Baker, *Saving Our Kids from Delinquency, Drugs, and Despair*.
New York: Cornelia and Michael Bessie Books, 1991. Good
chapter dealing with the relationship of unemployment and
teen crime; excellent index.

Karen Kinnear, *Violent Children*. Santa Barbara, CA: ABC-CLIO,
1995. Helpful handbook that includes invaluable reference
material for teachers and other professionals interested in edu-
cating others about the consequences of violence in the United
States today.

Rita Kramer, *At Tender Age: Violent Youth and Juvenile Justice*. New
York: Henry Holt, 1988. Readable account of what it's like for a
young offender being processed through the juvenile justice
system.

Neil Postman, *The Disappearance of Childhood*. New York: Delacorte
Press, 1982. Good description of the ways in which the media
might be contributing to the rising aggression and violence in
young people today.

Lois Warburton, *Prisons*. San Diego, CA: Lucent Books, 1993. Very
readable section summarizing current ideas on how prisons
might be changed.

Index

About the Author

Gail B. Stewart is the author of more than eighty books for children and young adults. She lives in Minneapolis, Minnesota, with her husband, Carl, and their sons, Ted, Elliot, and Flynn. When she is not writing, she spends her time reading, walking, and watching her sons play soccer.

Although she has enjoyed working on each of her books, she says that *The Other America* series has been especially gratifying. "So many of my past books have involved extensive research," she says, "but most of it has been library work—journals, magazines, books. But for these books, the main research has been very human. Spending the day with a little girl who has AIDS, or having lunch in a soup kitchen with a homeless man—these kinds of things give you insight that a library alone just can't match."

Stewart hopes that readers of this series will experience some of the same insights—perhaps even being motivated to use some of the suggestions at the end of each book to become involved with someone of the Other America.

About the Photographer

Twenty-two-year-old Natasha Frost has been a photographer for the *Minnesota Daily*, the University of Minnesota's student newspaper, for three and a half years. She currently attends the University of Minnesota and is studying sociology and journalism.

When not working at the paper or going to school, Frost enjoys traveling. "It gives me a chance to meet different people and expand my knowledge about the world."